Selected Poems

Selected Poems
1968–1998

John Wood

★ ★ ★

The University of Arkansas Press
Fayetteville
1999
★

Designed by Liz Lester

⊗   The paper used in this publication meets the minimum requirements
of the American National Standard for Permanence of Paper for Printed
Library Materials Z39.48-1984.

LIBRARY OF CONGRESS CATALOGING-IN-PUBLICATION DATA

Wood, John, 1947 Jan. 2–
     [Poems. Selections]
     Selected poems, 1968–1998 / John Wood.
          p.   cm.
     ISBN 1-55728-559-4 (cloth : alk. paper). —
ISBN 1-55728-560-8 (pbk. : alk. paper)
     I. Title.
PS3573.05946A6   1999
811'.54—dc21   98-54664
                                               CIP

for
Dafydd

who restores what time has taken

★ ★ ★

ACKNOWLEDGMENTS

Grateful acknowledgment is made to Paul Zimmer, the best friend my work has had, the kindest of souls, and the publisher of most of my books, including both *In Primary Light* and *The Gates of the Elect Kingdom*, which contained the first appearance of many of these poems; to the editors of the following journals in which others first appeared: *Antaeus, Body Politic, Cultural Vistas, The Kansas Quarterly, The Pacific Review, Poetry, Poetry Now, The Review, The Southern Review, Swallow's Tale;* and especially to the editor of *The New Orleans Review*, who was kind enough to publish "The Gates of the Elect Kingdom" in its entirety; to my friend Matthew Silverman who gave me the idea for "Remembering Madame Beausoleil"; to Mary Vaughan, another friend, for a more careful and exact eye than my own; to the Louisiana Division of the Arts which awarded me its Artist Fellowship for 1996–97, a fellowship that allowed me to have the summer of 1997 free to work; and finally to my brilliant editor and friend, Brian King, who saved me from more than one embarrassment.

CONTENTS

The Bitter Part of Heaven

They're all there: the man killed
by the pinball machine; the girl
who laughed to death; the dieting boy
who choked on a tapeworm wiggling up
in search of cakes and steak; and, of course, the babies—
the ones the ants, the mad chefs,
the anacondas, piranhas, and the threshing machines got.
This is heaven's bitter part
where all the dead from the *Enquirer*'s pages
are housed whole again but in anger
at irony and excess. Their eyeballs
have turned right again, hacked heads
have found their proper bodies, the mountains
of dog food ground by angry sons
or husbands have reconstituted.
But they brood and play out of tune,
pluck the wrong strings and frown
at those no tabloid ever eulogized.
It is hard for them being here
even though it's heaven,
things having gone quite wrong once,
irony having intruded
into an ordinary afternoon
like a steering wheel through the chest.
Some even say they would have done things
differently, things like sex, things
like that had they known it would have come to this:
a joke's butt reassembled with wings;
gowns of gossamer and gold stitching but a body
smooth as a mannequin's; a feeling of having been
betrayed. In other neighborhoods, others

who lived in fear of surprise,
waited on infected toenails and meteors,
the doors of saunas and freezers,
and then died boringly, old,
and on time, unable even to be surprised
that there was no surprise, fumble
through their songs like beginners,
though some have been at it for centuries.
They are distracted and equally bitter,
would have done things differently, too.
Of course, there are some areas
where hymns herald out of every window,
but there are few houses there
on those spare streets.

The Perils of Beauty

Pretty girl like lap dog—sometime go mad.
from *Charlie Chan in Rio*

No doubt a fair face, a fine
high bosom, or some glorious
buttocks' miraculous curve
has crazed down to bedlam
many a beauty, foamed up her lips,
snarled her smile, and snapped her mind
as easily as a string bean breaks
in the fingers of the kind of woman
whose mind is always safe, who now sits
on her porch, rocking beside
a heaped bushel, snapping
her supper and tomorrow's canning.

That beauty's peril lies beyond
any skeptic's doubt, beyond
the conundrums of cool, inscrutable sages,
is historical, incontestable, in Shakespeare,
and in her memory now as she sits
snapping beans and thinking about Raybella Skillen
and how Raybella used to comb her long brown hair;

she'd stand on her front porch combing it out
and the sun would strike it and everyone knew
that every husband wanted to put his hand deep
into Raybella's long brown hair and Raybella knew
and would say things like, "Keeping a neat head of hair
is the least you can do for your man," or "The Good Book says
a woman's hair is her crown and glory."

But one day Raybella wouldn't stop combing,
wouldn't go back to her kitchen, her green beans
and salt meat, and they boiled away and burnt
and ruined the pan, and at nine o'clock
she was still combing, and at ten o'clock
women were talking to her, but she just combed
and combed and stared at the sun,
and they had to go get her husband.

"Raybella's gone off the deep end,"
she remembered telling Mr. Skillen
as she snapped another bean now
and thought about how Jesus handled things,
handled them just about the same way she would.

The Comeback of Yma Sumac

El reino muerto vive.

Neruda

For decades now her voice, aureate
as Incan gold or the high, hidden cities
of the Andes, lay lost, silenced
by the fad affairs of our fickle ears,
while Yma, in the footsteps of Zog
and Zita, Hapsburgs, and Hohenzollerns, Yma
like some exiled, downcast, once-crowned head, waited
tables or washed the remains of rich sauce
from the plates of men with short memory
and oblivious to wonder, men who could not see
in the polished tines' revealing light
the purple touch and genealogies of grace,
or perhaps Yma simply stared out a window
and watched a world rushing away from the voluptuous days,
but now Xtabay has descended pentecostal
upon us again and Yma sings in Manhattan
and the crowds begin to remember and roar.

To live in a time freed from history's drift
is solace of sorts. Nothing gone stays gone
forever. The dead return, the forgotten
are recalled, the disgraced revised, washed clean,
their crimes bleached bright and pure: Nixon
turns elder statesman; Petain, a savior;
Mussolini whispers "Et tu"; and Judas
is canonized—all necessary saints.

History as history was
is all that's finally gone,

5

and in its tumble down and clutter
we've found the scraps to cloak our dreams.
Everything is missed but disarrayed;
the past is repaved in pyrite, and nostalgia
gated in oyster shell. Everyone is worthy
and every yesterday regretted. History
no longer indicts, for in the terror of the present
is no fear of the past—or any future we might now
in this instant with casual savagery
be hurling into shape.

Cancer Talkers

There are those who love its details,
love them more than the bedroom chronicles
of neighbors and colleagues, whose eyes
widen and glow at the thought
of things big as grapefruits
growing within chests and rectums,
inside friends, movie stars, and even
the anonymous friend of the friend of a friend.
They wonder if the doctors got it all
and talk about the man just eaten up,
the one they just had to sew back together.
They wonder about his wait and whether
he smoked again now that it didn't matter.
They are troubled by bone marrow
and how it's moved, whether it's scooped out
with gleaming surgical spoons
or suctioned into glass tubes, whether
it looks like what they've seen in beef bones.
And they think long on bald women, those
whose hair the hot chemicals loosened from scalps
and whether they went alone
to the wig shop or were accompanied
by a friend who stared or wept. And, of course,
they think of how it would feel
to have a chest smooth as a child's. They talk
of mortgages and insurance, wonder
how the little ones will cope and what she'll do
now or how he'll get along without her.
Their days go by in this talk,
and sometimes at night they even dream of it.
They see it moving within them

like a little ghost, like a child
with a sheet over its head, and they are as frightened
as they were thirty or forty years ago when
that same child stepped from behind a tree
one evening as they walked home
thinking only of mother and dinner.
The ghost child's boo bled their tears
for hours of nights; now, the small swarming cancer
also cries boo, cries beyond recognition, deformed,
gouged out, withered, to a crisp, in cold blood,
and calls for snipers, creatures, nurse killers, and cannibals
to come join him beneath his raging, racing sheet.

Upon Reading in the Newspaper That a Man in Kentucky Had Cut Off His Hand and His Foot with Pocket Knives and Then Gouged Out an Eye In Order That He Might Go to Heaven

He sat on the sidewalk outside his house
looking at his bloody chunks.
He threw into shrubbery what once
had caressed the hard thighs
of pure and Pentecostal girls.
He kicked at half of what had brought him
to their rooms and trailers. With his one eye
he saw what no longer offended him.
And above his head he felt the air stir
like a rustling of huge birds, and he saw
a golden feather fall. And he knew
that he had been welcomed.
He heard celestial juke boxes
break forth from the red lips of cherubic girls
voiced in honey and gowned in see-through lace.
And they hard-rocked a stubbed and bloody pain
in the wonder-working power.
And having watched his arm and leg
gush like the garden hose he daily watered
his pole beans and collards with, he, too, knew
the magic and power of blood.
And feeling himself going, he could feel
his shoulder blades begin to grow
and push from his flesh and push with a softness,
a sweetness, a sense of flight.

On a Photograph I Found of Two Young Factory Workers Standing beside a Piece of Heavy Machinery and Inscribed on the Reverse "Sacred to the Memory of Friendship"

FOR JUSTIN CALDWELL AND ROBERT NIKIRK

Though they did not stand close to each other,
and though they stared from their machine
indifferently, distantly, I do not doubt
they'd known each other's arms and fears.
The mustached one wore a small ring
on his little finger, and neither smiled
as that instant sacred to the memory
was snatched from a factory in Wilson, Kansas,
back when my grandparents were children.
And I saw that the one who'd inscribed it
had pasted on a prescription from F. Zeman, Druggist,
made out for the "Worst Kind of Poison."
And I could imagine how the other
laughed the way friends or wives
laugh at such love-clear jokes.
And I could see him, who, like his friend,
had never read Whitman or Plato or given thought
to the theories of passion, take him,
and kiss those quiet lips
and move his hands over his chest and back and thighs
until they both rememorized their love.
And perhaps they rested with a shot of whiskey, a beer,
and talked of the foreman or next Sunday's
lesson on Deuteronomy and what to do
with the extra tomatoes they'd grown,
the talk of those who've come to count

10

tomorrow assured. And perhaps one said,
"But if we get bad rain this year,
we won't have enough tomatoes to put up."
And the other said, "Maybe you're right;
it'd be a shame not to have enough for winter."
And they talked on like this into days and days
until finally there was nothing:
a house, a cane, an empty bed,
a few jars of juice, a photograph   waiting.

Remembering Madame Beausoleil, the Science Teacher at St. Dominic's Boys' Academy

For four years her voice,
powerful as telescopes
and cyclotrons, radium
and the equations of energy, lured them
with a gravity they did not understand.
When she would half smile
at their fumbled formulas,
their slide rules pulled too far,
they thought of women in movies
standing below the Eiffel Tower
smoking black cigarettes,
and they dreamed of girls, not the ones
they took to the proms, but girls
the lucky boys found
bulging through soft sweaters, girls
who went to drive-ins,
who danced slow and taught their sisters
how to kiss.

When Madame flipped her hair back
and put her hands to her waist,
when she would say, "Now my boys,
I tell you of a great genius,"
every unlucky boy felt love's poverty.
In their empty evenings,
dwarfed by the orbits of Newton,
of Kepler and Galileo, they read their lessons,
those expositions of universal law,
and later lay alone in their beds
in the toss and tumble

of terrestrial motion
and thought of heaven
and the way her breasts swayed,
thought of the spaces between the stars,
shapes and patterns intricate
as the lace of her blouse,
but finally thought
only of night and extinguished stars,
sleep and a gathering of emptiness
terrible as the savage shadow
her unfulfilling form could cast.

A Visitation

Years after I'd sealed their entry,
killed them by the hundreds,
and tombed up their queen,
others would still return
swarming in the waxen geometries
of instinct held there
between the roof and ceiling
of a sun porch, return to hum and spin
at what once had opened
into chambers of genius and comb.

I regretted everything,
had tried smoke and advice,
even called the honey man.
But I had a small son
and was tired of stings
and the sweet ooze falling
through the breaks
and knots of cypress
to spot our floor
and call out—even through walls—
the weaving lines of ants.

And then we forgot them
for four, maybe five years—
until this morning.

Forty or so had returned
to die on our door steps
near where once their ancestors
had entered a hive as distant to them
as some Knossos to me, driven

by magnetism and resonance
inexplicable as their love
of pollen, their need to comb
in serene and endless hexagons—
driven home—to their place—
to what they knew deep
in the labyrinths of their dancing
would be a welcome—
but which had so changed, so gone
that all the arteries of genesis
now fed back to no old country,
no ancestral comb, nor even
some silent, sour and alien heart,
but toward where we, too,
for no reason we know,
sightless storm.

Definitions

FOR JOHN METOYER

> *"Let my lusts be my ruin, then, since all else is a fake
> and mockery."*
>
> Hart Crane, July 7, 1926,
> letter from the Isle of Pines

They define us,
are the *veritas* of *vino*,
the *why* of *Why'd I do it?*
They're who we really are.
And they never let us forget it.

You cultivate a life of self-control,
propriety, probity, and so forth.
It can fall away in the twinkling
of someone else's eye; a whiff
of gin, perfume, or even certain sweats!;
the sight of hidden hairs and swells and breaks—
or a platter of glistening pork
heaped high as blood pressure can go;
can fall in the thousand other irrationals
of desire, for none's too bizarre
not to ruin someone's life. Donne knew reason
was a worthless viceroy, a useless
bureaucrat. It's fear alone—
the clap, the chair, cholesterol and cancer—
has the strength to restrain
when eyes, mouths, and groins go off.
But even their grip
is like the beach-party weakling's,
the old sand-kicked stutterer,
when some Atlas of lust comes flexing by,

because we know we'll be careful;
won't pick up anything; will stop
after the third; won't buy a whole carton;
and will take a long walk tomorrow.

We might as well admit
we're thralls to things invisible—
not Thrones nor Powers,
not angelics of any kind—
but sprites like pheromones, sweet ruts
we never sense we smell
but roll upon like dogs on turds,
hormonal tides that wash us
clean of all good sense, of all
the cultivars of grace, of everything
but guilt, regret, and guile.

We are the senses' indulgence, what they grew
to please themselves, toys
of smell and taste,
that sweet and senseless shiver
a thousand thousand saints
have said they've known
but called by other names.

The Correct Answers

to the newspaper's "Christmas Quiz about Europe" should
go like this:

1. "A customary Christmas Eve dish in Finland is
   made of . . .
       c) beans and franks."
2. "For hundreds of years, Spaniards have followed
   Christmas Eve mass with . . .
       b) a nationwide slumber party."
3. "A traditional belief throughout Europe is that at
   midnight on Christmas Eve . . .
       d) cows converse."

We are all alike.
Everyone is alike.
Everyone
is always alike:
hope, the bitch slut of history,
repeats the heart,
and we all live out
the old Magi journey.

We sit and wait for the miraculous
as if some grace were our due,
or possible. We eat our beans;
we sleep; we dream
like Europeans on Christmas Eve
and wait the wonders,
hope they will dig themselves
into the time-twisting marrow
or shower down in angelics
of cash, or simply prolong
the long decay.

It's Christmas Eve
and I am in Arkansas
and will sit down tonight with family and eat;
and perhaps they will pray,
and then I will sleep.
And possibly
when I wake,
something will have happened,
will have descended
like gold or thighs
or even God, and I will be
lifted, lifted
like flaming judgments from hope:
joyed and graced,
calm as the eyes
of a Sienese saint.

The Canticle of End-Times

Assured of the end, of tribulation
and rapture, of the come-round hour,
she rises with the muscle of farmers
stirred by harvest doubts and the length of light.
She rises from a room as simple as the bun of her hair,
as simple as a boiled egg,
simple as lemon juice and warm tap-water.
She rises to the fields of sin
as she leaves a room made safe through icon:
above her bed, a young and calling god
come to knock at the heart's door; over her stove the same boy,
nailed, suffocating, beginning the long wait.
And in her purse heavy with salvation
she carries "Words for Modern Man"
arranged in the grammar of fear.
And she stands for hours handing them out,
for hours looking into faces already marked,
for hours reciting the theorems of apocalypse,
the canticle of end-times and the great judging.
And in the evenings when she returns to her room
her fingers dark with smudged ink,
she washes her hands and sits quietly for a while,
sits looking into the face of the dying boy,
and weeps slow, small tears
knowing that the beastliness has already begun.

The Kālī Yuga

At the end of the Kālīyuga, the period in which we are now living,
Kālī, the mother of the universe, will set its destruction into motion as
her consort the Lord of the Dance, the great god Shiva, in a whirling
ring of fire begins the dance that will destroy the world.

When Buddy Ebsen dies and goes to heaven,
he's going to dance for Jesus,
going to dance an old-time dance
like a hoe-down dance danced fast.
An angel may play a jug. And Jesus might
play his fiddle. And Buddy's feet
will tickle the clouds, and he'll dance and dance.
And after the gates are opened to him,
he'll dance down golden streets,
his toes and heels tapping the gold,
and the angel with the jug will follow him,
and so will Jesus. And Buddy will dance
and keep dancing and dance for them all.
And the hard, cold gold will not bruise
his feet for they will be like air,
and Buddy will dance for what would be
hours and hours if watches ran in heaven
and heaven ran on time. And other angels
will find themselves jugs, and archangels
will lay down their horns and pick up fiddles
to play along with Jesus playing for Buddy.
And they will all be happy, and Buddy
will dance on and on till God Himself
takes off His robes, puts on His overalls

and kicks His feet to dance with Buddy.
And God and Buddy will dance for a day,
a day in which the dance is all,
and God will forget His cranks and gears,
and things will spin till they spin away,
dancing and dancing like Buddy and God.

The Wastes of Resurrection

I'd rather not have to worry with heaven.

Wilfred Owen,
spoken to me in a dream

Heaven's where it's all back
together again, we're told,
where scattered meat and bone
unite to bring some soldier home
to a wife who waited a while,
then remarried, grew old and died.
What bed does God propose
to hold that doubled grief:
to die and wait, then find
that love's forgot—
or does He wed all three
to bed down in polyandry,
then tell the reglued boy,
fifty years maybe sixty, blown
from his desire and thrust, "She's dry,
and her new husband's ass has caved in;
try to make do; a walk might help;
the streets are paved."

Opie and the Apples

When the new kid moved to Mayberry and didn't want to go
fishing with Opie and called him "Dopey" because he said
he'd rather fish than steal apples and Opie asked Andy if
he could fight the new kid because he'd called him names
and Andy said "No "and how that just wouldn't be right neighborly
and how Op 'u'd just have to find something to like about
the new kid and so Opie stole some apples, too, and got
in trouble and it was a terrible mess and Aunt Bea cried
and cried and Barney wanted to take Opie to the woodshed
but Andy had a big pow-wow with ol' Op and Opie just finally
beat the shit out of the new kid who then went fishing with
Opie and decided Aunt Bea, whom he earlier had said looked
like a big-titted wart hog, was real pretty and that her
fried chicken was better than anything he ever ate and that
his snooty mother who never fried chicken was a selfish snob
and his father was just too rich and busy to love a little kid,
whose single but very large tear finally made that father see
he needed to take him fishing with Opie and Andy and made
his mother run to Aunt Bea's kitchen begging for her recipe;
so when all that happened on that typical Mayberry day,
I wondered what Andy did when he got horny and if Barney dreamed
of being locked in a cell with Andy and no one would let them out
and there was a big shower nozzle and Andy took lots of showers
'cause he said a man oughta stay clean and Barney felt happy,
happier even than when he patrolled the streets, and if Floyd
ever raised the price of a haircut or nicked an ear, and if
there were high-school kids in Mayberry, boys who reached
into the sweaters of girls and girls who ran their hands
over the tight zippers of boys, and if apples ever rotted
in Mayberry, and how loud the preachers got when they talked
of apples and Eve and disobedience and if when Opie learned

to masturbate he would think of this day on which he stole apples
and got in trouble and Aunt Bea cried and cried because she knew
he'd be at himself in a few years and that socks and sheets
would show his shame and there would be nothing,
nothing she could say to him and that pimples would rise
on his face and that he would find his hand in sweaters
and his tongue deep into the cleft of the world's imperfections.
And she wept and tore chunks from her hair
and gnawed her knuckles knowing there was not grace enough
even here, even in Mayberry, to seal the thighs of Eve.

How Little Lillian Found
the Lord and Served Him

Yet bitter felt it still to die deserted.
                              William Cowper

When Big Lillian saw how the spoiled corn
aborted her pigs, she got in her wagon
and went down to the drug store
and bought her some ergot to feed Little Lillian
who couldn't leave the boys alone.
"I just can't help myself, Momma,"
Little Lillian would say. "Don't Jesus do no good?"
Big Lillian would say, and Little Lillian would reply,
"No, ma'am, He don't." Mr. Verdue, the druggist,
understanding a request for ergot,
also suggested cottonwood. He said,
"Big Lillian, I usually always sell my ergot
with a little cottonwood, and some take
a touch of quinine powder too."
Big Lillian wanted it all,
but when he handed her the package,
she said, "Calvin, this ain't enough."
And so she got her enough
to burn Little Lillian's womb out,
which she did, but not before
Little Lillian had herself an ergot-idiot.
He had kinky hair and was brown as a potato, which pleased
Big Lillian because she could blame it on
Amalene, Old Eva's daughter, "just a terrible colored gal,"
who, she said, had just come back
to Pine Bluff from New York City to leave it
on Old Eva's doorstep and then go back

to her "musician" friend—played a clarinet—in New York City.
Since Big Lillian was a Christian woman
who knew Christian duty, white or colored,
and since Old Eva was far too old to care for any ergot-idiot,
she took it on. And Old Eva,
who was real happy with her new wagon,
never said a thing. Little Lillian took to praying now
and a year later got herself married to a Baptist preacher.
After he hanged himself because he couldn't get her pregnant,
she took to preaching too, acknowledged her ergot-idiot,
and paid five dollars to have his name changed legal
to Lilliansin. Then she and her little brown idiot
started traveling the gospel circuit.
He was five now and slobbered real bad.
She'd pull him up on the stage and say,
"See what I done. If Jesus can wash that away,
which He in His mercy has done, then He can wash away
what you done too. Jesus Hisself made this little colored idiot
as a sign of the times. Repent ye whores and harlots
lest He drive you from His temple. Hallelujah!"
Lilliansin had a little banjo he'd strum wildly
every time she said *Hallelujah!*
And all those awaiting revival, the full taste of guilt's gall,
would stir at his banjo's twangs, stir from mutterings and dance
into the full vocabulary of seizure and ecstasy,
and Little Lillian grew rich and richer
and settled down and built herself a tabernacle
and married a God-fearing man she'd saved
in a truck stop on the outskirts of Albuquerque.
But along the way she lost her little idiot,
no longer preached about him. In fact,
everybody seemed to forget about him
after she said he went off to dentist school.
And Little Lillian and the man she met at the truck stop

started the Christian Radio Club
and in five years had saved enough souls
to open CRC Bible College right next to her tabernacle.
And Little Lillian was president for years,
president so long she forgot who Jesus was,
thought He might have been a little potato-colored idiot,
so long the college had to change its name to CTVC Bible College,
so long her toenails turned inward,
and her bowels stopped and she seemed to grow
smaller and smaller until she was hardly there,
hardly as big as a pea or a splinter
from the Cross, so small and lost
in the blue waves of her blankets, lost,
drifting, and as castaway as her sin.

Jam

The farmer's wicked wife does not put
cracklings in the farmer's cornbread.
At night she does not ask him
if he wants to use her.
She's never cleaned out the cistern,
and she often puts eggs in the ice box
that she's not wiped off.
The farmer begs for children;
his wife giggles silently.
And under the brown canvas of revivals
the Holy Spirit moves her pelvis and tongue
with the eating fire of quicklime.
And the other wives listen
as her egg-smooth lusts are confessed
and forgiven. Her testimonies to their husbands'
abilities with tractors and ropes, the breaking
of sod tight as their muscles
do not please them. They do not please
her sweating husband whose lips
twitch into smiles that are not smiles.
Though the revival man
who lays on the hands quivers for her confessions
and her hot bread and jams, her thick white hominy
and breaded steaks. And in his unknown voice
which she alone understands and moves her tongue to,
he begs for more in the name of Jesus, sweet Jesus.
And the daily read and curling pages
of her husband's Bible are thumbed
in the sweat of fear. And the wives sweat

in the sweat of fear and think they hear
the sound of wasps. But their slim husbands
sitting in open-necked shirts
only watch her God-touched hips
and feel breezes blowing through the rapture-rank tent.

How I Tried to Explain the Certainties of Faith and Petrunkevitch's Famous Essay on the Wasp and the Tarantula to a Pentecostal Student Worried about My Soul

He told me how he'd prayed,
besought God with Habakkuk's fervor,
and how into those prayers I
like some prodigal had come
and stood in their heart,
naked and ignorant, wobbling
on a rapturous balance
unaware, blind to the hand
and script which declared me
weighed and wanting, deaf
to the timbrels of angels
gliding as if they were rounding
again and again a gold and glowing rink.
Then Jesus, blonder now than ever,
his robe open slightly, his pectorals
hard as hatchets, his thighs
glistening, appeared saying,
"That man dreams of whores
and hacking them up. Go ask
after his soul." And so, he'd come,
but now wept and bit at his hands,
reached across the desk, took my hand
and kissed me, pressing hard his tongue.

Still holding his hand, I told him
my soul was well, that I would hack
no one, and had little use for visions,
but that Christ worked the world

like a wasp, worked it in a catching
and planting; that the sting, the seeding,
the final devouring *was* the Jesus-journey,
the whole point, the point of anything—
the point of inexplicable need
or the commands of a glistening god—
and the price, the price
even pagans pay, the price
to charge away profane uncertainty.

About Their Father's Business

For he is of the tribe of Tiger.

Christopher Smart, from *Jubilate Agno*

1. Discoveries

It was not Brendan's hand that drove the oar
Or held the helm, not Brendan's eyes
That mapped his way, nor Brendan's prayer
That blessed the sea's great gleaming subtleties.

No ordinary thing set him
To strike the ogham onto stones
And cross and bless the new world's rim
Or take the savage in his arms.

At the red pivot of his heart
The Christ-lion crouched and spun,
Purred round love's axised torque
And compassed him till it was done.

2. Visions

*As Louis Wain's madness grew, his art became increasingly inspired.
Santa cats held small haloed tabbies before wise cats bearing gifts, while
others grew so bright and geometric, their fur so dazzling, they were
indistinguishable from light.*

He dreamed the second coming, dreamed it
quickened with cottonwood and come too soon,
dreamed it finally flung to an ink pot's lip—
a weight, a ball, a pen-point's shimmering.

And he awoke in anger's sweat
to tell us how the fetus held

until it drank its weight of blustered blab
and then went out.

And on that same thorn-dazzled day,
crouched at anger's sullen shrine,
he saw what prowls the festered air
and holds the storm's still silent eye:

the quivering haunches' burnished blur, the spring,
the leap, the incandescent fur.

3. Questions

Did Curley really die because Larry
and Moe hit him in the head so much?
Did something happen backstage one night
at the Mickey Mouse Club?
Why do comic strips exist?
Who eats Spam?

Oh, if I could only know the answers,
I'd slip into the long, rare robes
of the Magus, and as Sirius rose
with the sun, I'd blend honey
with chokeberry and mercury.
I'd refine plasters, distill the draughts,
and administer them as balm and wine,
having come round to the knowledge
of important things, the knowledge
of what offends me, is maggot to me.

The bald head was slapped so much
I heard that it caved in one day
and Curly stumbled as Larry and Moe
jumped up and down. And I heard

that in the studio one night
behind the big mouse head,
a certain man—old, mustached—
lifted her sweater and hugged her
until she said, "If you're gentle."
And someone told me that Spam
went well with eggs
and B. O. Plenty, Terry, and Abner, and all of them
on Sunday mornings before church,
that it even tasted like the corned beef
Jiggs always dreamed Maggie might let him have.

This is what I have been told,
but I am wandless and robeless,
unable to kill or redeem you
being neither lion, star, nor mage.

But you should know
that I have heard a rustling in the night,
the slow stalk of massive paws,
and smelled musk's high anger on the air.

Expulsions

. . . in the nineteenth century backwoods farmers in the U.S.A digging up a thighbone taller than a man feared they had found the bones of the fallen angels.

Nancy Newhall

He often thought of them,
those storms of flaming trash
falling
back in that turning world
before the land was done,
thought of them and feared
the humor of his God,
feared He might be fat,
feared He laughed,
that He laughed
like a fat boy with firecrackers,
that Adam, wingless now
and always falling, was the joke—
monkey lust in angel grace—
and that we too were shaped
for ruin, ordained
for danger and dark curves.

And on his tongue he smelled
the stench of wings
wrathed to pitch. He wept
at what he furrowed out:
teeth like fists,
great pelvic shards, coal
that once held thighs
curved with risks.

And he'd cut wings
on planks for markers
and put them there and there
and there till the fields failed
and he forgot his fears—
of birds, of locusts, of thick grubs
glowing at the roots, curving
them like thumbs, and even
a neighbor's tongue in the mouth
of his wife and down and along
the curves of his wife,

because the fields were sanctified,
made holy by his hand. And he
in glittering arrogance arose
and went out, redug
the smoothest bone and lay down
beside it, watched it
finally now and at last
flesh out.

And he was down and in love,
and it was like Babylon,
tiered gardens and the smell
of cedar, of curves and danger.
And he lay there copulating
with the air until the noise
of the wolves grew louder
than the thoughts he could think,
louder than her splendid sighs.

Baptisms

When he spoke of revelations,
his voice covered her
like anointings, and she knew things,
knew God was in his tongue,
on his lips, shining
on the gold, and way down
where sound started, knew
he was right, like before,
like when he said
she wouldn't bleed
when her mole came off,
Jesus having already bled
the afflictions of organs
out, the sins of the flock
out, and how her blood
was cleansed of cancers, cleansed
before she was even born,
cleansed in Judea
when the veil was rent.
And she remembered his fingers
in the hair under her arm
and how he felt the mole, how
when he rolled it back
and forth between his thumb
and forefinger, rolled it slowly
whispering "Jesus Jesus," she
had to take deep breaths.
And she wished for a talent,
for something special she could do,
like tool his name in Old English
to the back of a belt.

And especially now because
he was right, because
God was all over him, because
when he was close and down
in your face praying, you could smell
his breath, and it was like bread,
and he was saying heaven would be withheld
from those baptized in water alone,
for where were the nails,
the Judas baptism of iron,
and where was the spoiling fire
of harrowed hell's cleansing.
And she knew he was right.
And on Monday she went out
and bought nails and dynamite
and filled her car, and she thought
of him and on Jesus, on the pig iron
and flames, and she remembered Jesus saying
to suffer the children, and then
she was sure she was sure,
and it was like rainbows arcing,
and she was on her way.

Conversions

*Well, my marriage finally did fall apart and I lost the house, but I am
really happy now; it all led me to Him. John, believe me, He's the real
sweetness and light.*

I've seen a crippled lust prod men
toward Christ with the fire they could not make,
heard the tabernacles of hysteria shake and timbrel forth
the things the flesh would not release,
smelled sin glow bright as halos in the scalps' grease,
and watched the spittled foam
bead at the praising, stuttered edges of speech,
until smoldering in the impotent auras of despair, they were at last
consumed. I've watched the bolted embrace of marriage
rust over and disengage in a sharding down, and seen them then
rise, but to no more than a wafer's reach. And I've stared
at the lunatics whipped and dancing their rapturous hosannas,
their eyes luxurious with tears, with the ecstatic fruit
of thorn and nail.

It is impossible not to notice, impossible
to avert the eyes where frenzy spins
and whole congregations run leaping before you
like plagues, brown and biblical.

But who can say I'd not be as touched and springing,
my sight as furiously gazed, my tongue as thick and gabbled,
were I to lose my son, and this flesh of mine empty out all joy.
The skin of even me, then, might be animated
by where despair had pushed so far, might be quickened
                and convulsed.

I wished him well but prayed
for calm repose and empty sky,
that I might never know
the whirling psalms of such peace,
his starred and honeyed bliss.

Theological Meditation

At the heart of the wood
lie only the loins' sweet shudder
and a wide white sleep,
smooth and polished as glazed snow.

And for no more than that
we fret and flame,
risk the body's wreck
and the mind's fire going:
all to mumble our greed toward . . .

what? an emptiness
shaped like our own confounding flesh;
or worse, some deified orifice,
a function of blood and muscle,
the residue of instinct
left piled and steaming
at the cave's back
deep in Neanderthal dark?

But were the mystery solved
and all saw the plotless pages,
the million picaresque years,
would any ring of men then dance
in supple time, lift voice in chant,
or frame ritual from frenzy,

or would the rhythms rise
flush and foaming to rally
old enmity and the groin's random temper
to new purpose—certain this time,
blood-bright, and malign?

Angelic Revelation

1.

My angel is my fortune—and the mystic made real.
No old beard stalking heaven with sticks
of crackling lightning in his hands,
storming at pig meat, menstruation, and buggery,
appeased by burnt lamb, by foreskins heaped into high piles;
no seductive boy, skin like cinnamon,
muscular as a carpenter and capable of magic;
nor any bliss nor terror they promise
haunt my habits and days.

Yet I do know angelic orders guard, know
they *alone* are *all* that choir and chorus us
through the dark between the stars.

2.

They wing down in scents to hold and stagger us
from dangers common senses cannot sense—
to let us know that fathers passed from flesh
have not passed from us.

They descend in dreams, the winged mares
of warning, and fall as revelation
before the closed eyes of sleep
descending to advise and keep.

Or they come gowned in glories,
wide bolts of light,
full-fleshed and guiding,
navigating the stellar night.

3.

Within the body the angel unfolds
to hover naked and radiant
there in heaven's profane parameters
erect in the compass of flesh,
glowing beyond the degrees of gold or shame or inlaid pearl,
unfolds to reveal heaven, too, is real,
self-given as grace and self-ordained,
unfolds to sing salvations out in rose and pear and cinnamon,
in cautions called from sleep and visions given shape,
unfolds for us to see the heart-star revealed,
the heart's light swell, the dark dispelled.

Garden Walk after Looking
at a Lacquer Box by Zeshin

I wander onto the sun-struck stones
of the garden and weave between rows
of basil and rose, of laurel and ginger,
of mint and things without scent as well,
all bright leaved and petaled,
through arbors vining with the smell
of women and warmth, and toward the pond
where I sit and toss meal
into the dazzled water and watch
the red scales of fifty fish flash
as they take food, submerge, and rise again.

And in the shadows of leaves,
the reflected limbs of pecan and oak,
following slight movements, counting
the dragonflies dipping to drink,
wasps dipping to drink, their minute circles,
the occasional slow, descending leaf
in the still, warm, and motionless air,
I watch the inconsequential clutter of things,
the random jumbles that trance and mesmer us
with the same authority as those clutters
which connect into consequence,
transform into metaphor,
which insist, firmly as a father,
a map's fragment, an old book—
insist with no right in the matter
our lives upon us.

Flemish Scene

In the foreground
snow fell like down
over Flanders,
over the moon-brushed town,
nightcapped the tops
of trees, rubbed white
the market's bricks,
and finally flecked
the panes of glass
from where the warm
and ambered glow
of burning wax
kept the light
for linen men
whose hands stacked up
their yesterdays,
and for cooks
who scrubbed their copper down
and plucked the feathers
from fattened geese.

But in the background,
removed, toward the edge,
so near exclusion and eclipse,
luminous lambs
lay silent, staring,
their keepers dumbed
at such starred
and nimbused light,
at wizard kings
in gaudy glitter
bent down to offer up

the honey bright
and fragrant signs
the hungry stars required,
sureties they'd brought so far,
carried with fear and care,
carried from the spiced and domed,
the silken, star-driven,
the sacrificial and devouring East.

Withdrawal and Return

FOR CAROL, AT YULE

> *"Everything we now see as beauty was for the Celts religion. . . .*
> *This . . . brought about . . . the relentless attacks of saints and*
> *missionaries on those beliefs and practices of the past they could*
> *not incorporate into Christian ritual. Thus in the fifth century St*
> *Martin of Tours ordered that a much revered pine tree should be cut*
> *down. . . . those who held to the old ways . . . lamented the coming*
> *of this new religion that practiced such sacrilege. . . ."*
>
> William Anderson in
> *Green Man: The Archetype*
> *of our Oneness with the Earth*

When Martin felled the pine,
the modern world began to sing.
Christ wintered in
and fields went brown.
The grail of gall began to rise.

Bitter clouds blocked and held
and broke the light.
Stones that had for centuries
clocked the seasons' turn
shadowed down in fractured time.
Apples would not fall,
and larks forgot their flight.
Rainbows crumbled in the air.
The oracles of groves and fields
fell back to seed and went to sleep.

But now the church has lost its will
and history's veil is pulled back—
the heaps of bone revealed.
Times have turned,

and fields are fluent once again.
Eloquent in ancient tongues,
they turn and bend the corn,
bend it back to oracle,
to the syntax of seasons,
the gestures of leaves,
the four voices of Her voice.

And now the clouds unlock.
The prayer of corn begins to stir the earth.
And larks and hymns uplift
to ready forth the land.
Seeds long locked in anger break.
The holy pine begins to rise.
And everything is rising now,
rising green and waiting.

The Gates of the Elect Kingdom

FOR PAUL ZIMMER

Bless the man who can restore the spirit.
Wilhelm Johannes Hoade

I: Proem

I originally considered subtitling *The Gates of the Elect Kingdom* "An Historical Poem" because it is based on historical characters, historical events, and what is certainly one of the great visionary moments, probably the last of such moments in pre-War, mid-nineteenth-century America—the founding of the Hoadeite community in Kansas. In fact, the story of Wilhelm Hoade, his visions, his coming to America, and the establishing of his community is a compact American epic comprising all the best and most hopeful dreams of pre–Civil War America.

In the poem I have tried to be faithful to those characters and events; however, at times I have, of course, manufactured dialogue, minor details, and so forth, but at no point is there anything in the poem that could not have actually happened or is unfaithful to the history or the teachings of the Hoadeite movement. In fact, many of Hoade's own words—except those in the *Vision* poems—are taken from Hoade's *Mysteries*, and even the *Visions* are influenced by the descriptions Hoade gave of them and that were recorded by his followers after his death. The historical facts of the Hoadeite movement are fairly well-known and even entered the American artistic consciousness in the 1930s and 1940s with Aaron Copland's ballet suite *Seven Hoadeite Dances* choreographed and danced by Martha Graham and Rockwell Kent's beautifully illustrated edition of Hoade's sermons, *The Mysteries*, published by the Limited Editions Club.

Wilhelm Johannes Hoade (1788–1852), founder of the Family of the Elect Kingdom, known as the Hoadeites, was born in Germany and emigrated to the U.S. with his followers in the mid-1840s. They established a vaguely socialistic-messianic agricultural community of about one hundred individuals near Manhattan, Kansas, where they believed Jesus's return would occur in 1857. Hoade died in 1852, but the community continued to flourish until 1858 when the members began deserting it. By the end of 1859 all but Adolphus Winkler, one of Hoade's original *Twelve Elect*, in whose name the actual deed to Kingdom Farm passed on Hoade's death; Winkler's wife, Alma; his two daughters, Eva and Clara; and their husbands had also departed.

For readers interested in more information, probably the best work on the subject is Paul Kettle's *The Hoadeite Community at Kingdom Farm* (Manhattan: Kansas State University Press, 1958). Nedie Lyon's essay on "Hoadeite Hymnody" in the January 1932 *American Choral Journal* is also quite interesting and important because it influenced Copland's ballet and is still probably the best work on the musical life at Kingdom Farm. Occasionally rare pieces of Hoadeite folk art appear on the market, most notably was a beautiful Hoadeite Wedding Cup consigned to Sotheby's in 1962 (see *Historical Americana*, Sale 1001, May 25, 1962, lot 33, photograph on p. 64), of which only two others are known, one at the Walker Museum at Kansas State University and one at the Wilhelm Hoade House in Manhattan.

My interest in Hoade as a subject for a poem is actually an outgrowth of my scholarly work in early photographic history. I have published several volumes on the daguerreotype, the first photographic process, and almost anyone who has studied the literature of this process has encountered both the name and visage of W. J. Hoade. While the well-known St. Louis daguerreotypist John Fitzgibbon (see my *The Daguerreotype* [Iowa City: University of Iowa Press, 1989], p. 120 and plate 14) was in Kansas making his famous series of Indian portraits, he happened to take a picture of Hoade which has been reproduced many times. Fitzgibbon even left a short record of the sitting in an article entitled "Daguerreotyping" which appeared in *The Western Journal and Civilian* 6 (1851), pp. 200–203, 380–385. He wrote, "After leaving the camp of Kno-Shr, I traveled to the Hoadeite community near Manhattan, having read of Herr Hoade and his Elect Elders in the press, a fact of which I informed him upon our introduction. . . . When I suggested he pose standing, for Hoade was an extremely large man, and holding a Bible, as it is the common manner to pose with the instruments of one's trade, he replied, 'Mr. Fitzgibbon, what you read about me in your papers must surely have been inaccurate. I fear you do not know me at all,' whereupon he placed the beads I had presented him around his neck, took up a sickle, a handful of wheat, crossed his arms, sat down in the posing chair, and said, 'Now, Sir, you see me as I am.'" The power of that portrait and the quirkiness of Hoade's response intrigued me.

Hoade's importance was probably best summed up by F. R. Leavis in his *Scrutiny* essay "Mythic America: Peaceable Kingdoms and Utopian Visions." He wrote, "Compared to Young and the Mormonian Latter-Day Saints of Utah, Hoade's Elect were failures; compared to the Shakers, their craft-work was bizarrely baroque; compared to Robert Owen, Hoade was no true 'reformer'; but considering them all and compared to them all, his *vision*, simple and beatific, was, without doubt, the most visionary."

II: A Vision of Kansas

And He came unto me saying, *Wilhelm,*
rise up from the abundance of the Rhine
for I will wither down its grape, for I
will scatter out its vine, for I will dream and sow
its furrows dry with fireless flint
that will not strike a wine for Elect lips:
an Elder's scriptured kiss or the plain mouths
of maids. And they shall turn and put their backs
in shunned disgust to all the Rhine and rivers of greed,
and they shall rise and bring their sickles cross a wheat
where lands lay down in gold and prosperings.
In the Christ-farm of a heart's bleak need alone
shall I be found, in the stubborn soil and the wheat's bright grain.
Rise; go.

And Hoade took up his atlas and knew
that God had called him to Kansas.

III: The Beginning of the Progress

He preached of the new world
and the exodus from the old,
and soon there gathered about him others
for whom the word *Kansas* was also
God-touched, fertile and shimmering,
awaiting their plows. And they sold
all they owned and bought passage.

I have wandered within the compass,
the elect and measured arc
of love's geometry; come hand in hand within
and hand in hand with me.
I've divined joy's pure theorem
to plot the equations of grace,
seen Christ aglow in the eye of the child.
Hand in hand we'll take up the plow
and build His Kingdom's farm on Kansas plains.
And Christ will come to harvest all our yield
Shoulder to shoulder plowing Kansas to Paradise.

IV: The Imminent Return and the Congress of the Elect

And Hoade spoke of the Millennial Congress
and the sacred year lost in Gregorian inaccuracy,
of 1857 and *The Imminent Return*:

Let the women be neglectful of the canning of beans,
their cooking, and all the stuff of kitchens,
but let them be combing with love,
setting the lightning of their high loaved hair into wifely gifts
and dreaming of husbands coming home bigger than Jesus;
let men be driven by the girl-lust
they cannot carve from their sight or cut

from their grip and gait; let girls
weep for rapturous rinks and angel-boys askate and sweating
round an erect and risen Christ; let the world
hunger for their preacher's yeasty breath, his rising hands,
the born-again moment immersed in Christ's ejaculant fire;
let the world convene
and take up their wounds and gather in congress
to announce the protocols of their anger; to issue
the drafts of their secession from centuries
of numbed control, from pyx and chalice
and all the vestments of shame; to indict
the long priesthood of self-castration;
to await the undoing of the past,
the breaking from high clouds of earthly canticles,
to await the slow fall of shuddered glories in bright shafts,
godhood mantling down in ripplings of Kansas light,
to await the Christ-herald of the rapturous hour.

V: The Injunction

> *Know history as you know the soil and the seed, the compass, the
> square and the beam, Christ's embrace and the hold of your love.*
>> Wilhelm Hoade,
>> *The Mysteries,* III, ix, 2

The man with no patience for history
is frightened of mold.
He constantly brushes the backs of his books
and watches husked corn as it dries in the bin.
He can feel the grit of its spores
as they grind and rise in the sockets of his hips,
or lace along a femur's length.
He smells it on his children's breath
and nightly fears he feels its dirt
curving round his wife's great thighs.

The man with no patience for history
longs for a Paradise halted as stone.
He shines his tomorrows bright to their burning
and guards his slipping hours,
but hours cannot slip in Kansas light,
cannot slip from fields of grain,
cannot slip in works of love.
And Paradise was never still.
The past's decay is future's hope.
And in this moment work and wait
and Christ will come and set you free.

VI: Melchior and the Butterflies

It was Melchior who first saw them,
Melchior who first heard them.
In the long hall of beds he lay
with the Elect dreaming of Christ
loading high the haywain,
stacking the abundance of Kingdom Farm,
and baking it into loaves; Jesus calling
for flour and milk, and the great white bowls
of brown eggs stacked so high children marveled,
and the children handing out the bright loaves,
and everywhere the odors of yeast and ovens,
of morning and fresh bread, but then
Melchior's dream turned with the odor of vanilla,
and he awoke, and vanilla was in the air
and everywhere, and up and down the long hall,
and he looked out, and it was as if
all the monarchs of Kansas had come,
as if Kingdom Farm could lift into the air.
And he awoke Hoade and the others
and together they walked in their smocks

through acres of butterflies. And butterflies
lit on their arms and in their hair, and Hoade wept
and understood. And in the evening they lifted,
but Kingdom Farm was drenched
for weeks in the rich dark secrets of vanilla.

VII: Divisions of Labor

I

Sometimes I tire of teaching
and think of the other women,
the ones in the kitchen
or those in the gardens
digging and planting. They get
all the praise—and daily!:
"Why I've never seen such fat cabbages"; or
"This sausage is better than any
I ever ate in München." That kind
of stuff. "Oh, Sister, your potatoes are like—"
angel turds, I thought; Christ, forgive me, but
that is what passed through my mind once
listening to some old Elder going on
to Sister Bertha. All I ever hear
are things like: "But why must we
speak English"; and "Why must we
read music"; or "I don't need geometry
to build a barn." Later they'll be glad
when their barns don't fall over,
and English and music are natural
as German. But by the time a learned thing
becomes second nature, the teacher is as forgotten
as first nature's long-gone tutor.
None will ever look back to Sister Anna

and beam as they would for a cabbage.
The group's greater good, the Kingdom's abundance, is,
I'm told—and retold, my dutied concern, but when they're all,
all so—so stupid, so stupid and rude,
a greater good is a difficulty to fathom,
harder even than a Paradise to come
on Kansas fields.

II

I must have mixed a whole tablespoon
of horseradish into Anna's portion
of sauerkraut yesterday. Those big
bright eyes of hers went red, the tears
ran, and she downed two glasses of water.
"What is it, Sister? Oh, Anna,
what is it, dear?" "Taste this, Bertha,"
she screamed, and the whole hall was looking on.
"Oh, Sister, I can tell by the smell
that some of the horseradish the other Sisters
were making must have fallen in your portion;
can't you smell it, too?" That was great fun.
She disgusts me with her ways,
her little harp and clarinet and perfect English.
She won't even use German when it's all us
together—talking privately of certain matters.
She with her little classroom all her own
and me in a kitchen shared with ten others,
and my little Hannes coming home and saying things
like, "Nein, Momma, Schwester Anna sagt
es ist pronounced best *doll-ar* not *ta-ler*."
Christ, there's not enough horseradish in Kansas
for her. I know I'm to love us all,
but love is no easy thing. And I seldom feel like Christ

chopping cabbage, stuffing sausage day in day out
and listening to the other women. I wish I had time
to sit down sometimes and just think—about anything,
or listen to my Hannes play his clarinet.

VIII: The Expulsion of the Heretics

They are as dangerous as wagons,
those intense, soft voices
clabbered up with flatteries
and what sometimes sounds
like desire. Such tones
could web away a man's
whole heart and drain it down
like a dry gourd on a vine;
yet they can look so sad
in their cast downs, so
St. Sebastianed, erect
with arrows, so St. Agathaed, breasts
laid out, the blind
would weep, the dumb stir
lips into low declamations,
and the long deaf hear again.
Oh, we've held them close
and paid in all the corn and currency,
the wealth of fields and vineyards,
paid in all the abundance the flesh
can negotiate. But now, here in Kansas,
they are gone, and let them stay,
and let us keep our lusts
and know them and be thankful,
but let desire's draining angels be gone,
gone to weave and web another place.
And in their scurried leavings,

see them as they are, see them grown brighter
and more proficient from our embrace, polished now,
bright as a cock's gaff, and glittering,
their red clocks gleaming, sanding down
another's days. And so, they've driven off—fire flung
from their wagons—toward orchards
or fields of berries or snow
or some preferable somewhere,
furious and sulking at how demanding
our wishes and needs, at how unfair
the terrible ordinances of love.

IX: Exultation: Melchior Tobit, the First Black Hoadeite, Leads the Service at Kingdom Farm on New Year's Day 1851

Little Babe Jesus don't let nobody sink
that'll grab the life line. No sir;
he don't let you sink. That little ol' baby hand
just gets a hold like a lover and pulls.
O Lordy how he pulls, that little baby. Why,
he the god of fire; he the shock; he the flambations
of the spirit, the burnations of love; he be love
all bundled up, the outlaw of love; the outlaw of love.
He come up from behind and stobs you
with his pearly knife of love, stobs you
in the ribs, and you feel love movin' then,
movin' like the Pentecost, movin' in your mouth,
in your shirt, in your pants, movin', movin' and you
want to scream and tell everybody about love.
Love makes the cats flex they whiskers
and the great whales leap for joy;
it makes the panthers shine at night

and the white rabbits dance in the light.
Love's the cocoon of fire.
And He the Betsy Ross spinner
of your soul. He the tailor
of your celestial suit.
Ooooh Jesus, take your scissors
and trim me till I be good enough.
O Lordy, dry my throat out
like the fish heads in the sun,
give me the fresh hot pig blood to drink,
give me the meat of castor bean,
the juice of unboiled poke to quench my sin.
Burn up my sin with your love.
Let me see into the lightning center
of your sight; burn out my eyes.
Ooooh Jeeesus, fisher man,
throw out your net and pull me in
and let me be worthy to be caught,
worthy to be set before you to break with bread.
Fix me on your holy spit and
turn me turn me turn me
till I'm worthy. O farmer god,
plow-master and driver,
drive me with the burning love.
Brothers, Sisters, do you feel it?
The god of fire,
the outlaw; the shock. And He love us all.
Makes no difference. He love us all.
Black and white and German and Indian
and cannibal, and head hunters too,
and all the children,
all the children of the world.

And Hoade arose and said,
Ah, Melchior, it is so; it is so.

X: Chivaree and Dance for the Marriage of Melchior and Carla

They clanged the pots; they clanged the pans;
they broke the dishes and rattled the cans;
they beat on the windows; they beat on the door
to chivaree Carla and Melchior.

But in their bed and deaf to the din,
he held, he touched, he took his bride,
glad for the lust they neither could hide,
glad for the shapes their shapes were in.

Within that dance of lust and gene,
desire's psalm of give and take,
they rose and fell for their bodies' sake,
like no waltz, nor reel, nor buck and wing, like no stepping
            they had seen.

And glad for the Lord of Love's entrancing,
the crowd outside began its dancing
to the strings and flutes and the golden harp,
all swinging and winging till the day twirled to dark.

XI: The Omega Vision

A Christ-storm of fire in a steepled field spinning,
God Himself thundering the rows of frenzied thorn,
His iron sandals' fall for a dance of thinning,
the black bloom of His frown, the graving of the ground.

That is what I told them,
and I did see Him, gigantic, frightening,
tearing through the corn
setting it ablaze as His robes, all pure flame,
touched the stalks. And I watched Him,

and He looked into my eyes.
And His hands
were like birds swooping
and tearing at those fat with sin
as if they were the harvest.
And the fields flamed-out in blood
and the blood drove the flames like whale oil.
And bones were crackling at His fingers' touch
like stormed branches in the wind.
And He said to me,
To make the Kingdom spring
will take the nailed and hammered joy of Jael.
Love me less and the kernel will not crack.

And He turned from me
and the hem of His fiery gown seemed to spin
and He began to spin, and I saw Him
lift and rise over the ruined fields,
saw Him rising, turning
turning into pure tornado.

XII: The Murder of Melchior

Hoade heard them from his study
calling out, saw the torches through his windows,
and he thought, *Has God sent me newly Elect?*
But going out, he saw into their eyes,
saw flung down at his door
what first in the darkness he thought
a smoldering log, till his eyes adjusted
and he smelled the burned meat of man.
"How you like your nigger now?"

Did you send me here for this, O Lord?
Is this the promised fruit of Kansas fields?

I swore no swords if love were shields
but will not bear a thing this hard.

And Hoade was like lightning reaching out
and he grabbed the man who spoke to him
and plunged his fingers through his eyes
and pushed him to the cold ground
and no one moved as Hoade held him there
and with his massive hands
pulled the man's face from his head
and flung it at the sweating, screaming,
still, unmoving mob.

XIII: Hoade's Return

> *"The Rev. W. J. Hoade of the Kingdom Farm community turned*
> *himself in to authorities last Tuesday night in regard to the death*
> *of Sean Cook, a baker, of Manhattan. Local magistrate Eliphalet*
> *Putnam released Hoade Wednesday morning saying there was 'just*
> *cause,' 'wrongs done on both sides,' and that 'lives of freemen are of*
> *equal value before the law.'"*
>
> The Manhattan Weekly Traveler,
> 8 February 1852

The hogs and hounds of a rotting god
could not drive me from Christ's own land,
and they've eaten my galled rebuke
and tasted Christ's command.
Under His iron sandaled fury
I've broken the breastbone of sin.
And for this, I am blest,
and Melchior is blest. And though torn
for such blessing, we are risen and radiant;
torn in the flaming trial

we have risen from the furnace whole,
weighed but not wanting
in the days that draw the stations of our blessing.

And now the sunflowers rise and sway for us.
I have watched them in the breezes
of evening, watched them swaying,
watched clouds driving over them
and smelled Christ's breath in the wind,
rich as vanilla.

Love and work will reconstitute the soil,
will fertile the ground for Harvest.
And we will heap high the long table with goods,
and He will return to sit with us and eat the corn,
and pork, pure and clean as doves,
and red cabbage cooked purple as a king's raiment.
And He will drink the cool, amber cider of our trees
in new communion.

He has fled from this glebe
and Beastmen now sow the beast seed.
We have looked into their faces,
seen them in the places we passed,
seen them at their trades
and innocence held harlot for gold.
Shame, shame smolders in the air.
We must tear the Beast mask from their faces
and uproot the thorns they've sown,
prepare the fields for Christ and the children's coming.

Sisters, Brothers, though I may not be with you at Harvest,
know that I am with Him, joined in the pit of the peach,
in the apple's core, in the onion's most layered chamber,

in the swaying heads of sunflowers, in their dominion
of the fields, and in their risings and upliftings over the children.
I will be with Him then, protecting
and awaiting you, awaiting you
in the sanctification of innocence.

XIV: Lament and Doubts

*There was one vision, the last, my sisters and brothers, that I shan't
reveal—and cannot understand.*

Wilhelm Hoade,
The Mysteries, Appendix A

That first night our wagons rolled into Kansas
butterflies descended
like shooting stars to lead us.
And they angeled us on for days, their bliss
and radiance pulling us, proving Christ attended
and blessed our progress.

We knew the soil would be stubborn as doubt
but the wheat's grain bright, that Christ Himself would help plow
the fields till they delivered up loaves
to lesson all the world in love's
arithmetic, and count love's sum as how
the sum of charity was reckoned out.

Did we stumble toward stars gone out
and swear to break a field of stone?
Could Christ allow such a fate
as Melchior's on a route
of angels? Did the road only lead to charred bone
at what I thought the kingdom's gate?

XV: Carla Tobit Tells the Women That He Is Gone

*"Hoade suffered a stroke while working in the cornfields and was
not found until late in the evening after he failed to arrive for dinner.
Carla Tobit and the Winklers sat at his bedside and were careful to
record everything he said as he passed in and out of consciousness
throughout the night. He died at precisely 6:00 a.m. on the morning
June 5, 1852."*

Paul Kettle, *The Hoadeite Community
at Kingdom Farm*, p. 258.

It was the first time I'd heard him speak in German for years.
It was as if he'd forgotten English, forgotten Kansas,
forgotten us all and everything. Brother Adolphus said
it wasn't Hoade but the stroke speaking,
that he'd so long lain outstretched in the sun and corn
his mind had gone. How else could the Harvest
slip from his lips, could the thought of His coming
and the bread we'd bake take flight.
But it had. Even when I spoke to him of Melchior
he didn't remember. He would just call for his mother.
Mutti, Mutti, he must have said a hundred times.
I thought there would be Words,
a final message, something to set down
or for the masons to cut, a testament.
But there was nothing. At the end he said,
Give me a sip of cider. And Sister Alma raised his head,
and he took a sip and said, *The core of the apple is bitter.*
Gibberish, I thought, but took it down.
And then he said, *Oh, it is so rich the room cannot hold it.
Open the doors; open the doors or the walls will break
with the sweetness.* And he breathed in deeply,
and there was nothing more,
and he was gone.

XVI: Waiting for Jesus

They waited from New Year's to Year's End
as expectation and disappointment rose to fill each day,
rose like the ripe sweet stench of silage
that hovered over the farm all summer.
Most thought it would be New Year's;
then that it would be Easter; and then, and then,
and on and on till finally at last on the Year's Eve
at midnight's wide eye's twinkling, they knew
in that sparkled turning He would descend
star-like upon the fields with light falling about Him
and night turning morning, and years and time all falling away
as clocks and calendars began again at noon in the year One.
And so they prepared the greatest feast they'd ever set:
pieces of comb were broken from the hive
heavy with honey and big as hands;
pigs were roasted and glazed rosy
with the jam of sweet plums from last canning;
and hot cabbage in wide wooden bowls
was shredded and sweetened and studded with caraway;
and jars of peaches, pickled and smelling of clove
and cinnamon stick, were opened and set out;
and the long table looked as it never had looked.
And the sisters went about their work
asking the questions they'd asked all year:
"What will you say to Him?" "What will you do
if He looks at you?" "What if He touches your hand
when you set His plate before Him?" And they worried,
"Will I be able to say, 'More cabbage, Lord? More pork?
Some cider for Your cup?'" And the men rehearsed their lines, as well:
"We've waited a long time, Lord; thank You for coming."
"Do You plan to shift the seasons, turn winter back,

to begin the planting now?" "Do You need a dray, Lord,
or will Your plow furrow though fields at Your touch?"
And "Forgive us our stupid questions, but this is so new, Lord;
we don't know how it is to work with You, or if we even
              need to speak."
But by six in the morning discontent and anger had set in,
the pork was cold and covered with a caul of grease,
the women had fallen asleep round the long table,
and von Tungeln, one of the original twelve,
said he'd had his doubts, that Hoade was false,
and he and his were heading westward. And rage broke out
like a fire in the corn and faces were dark as bruises
and others said they'd go with von Tungeln
or would just go. And they did and the end began,
and all Winkler's words couldn't stop it:
"Even prophets can misfigure,
but the Vision's still true.
Christ's still coming.
Why leave; life's good here."
But Winkler had no voice for prophecy
or magic and could hold few for long—
and finally none but his own, and they worked
what acres they could and still believed,
still waited, still sometimes picked up
the bright, sweet scent of vanilla on the air.

XVII: Emma Goldman Thinks of Hoade

"I had read The Mysteries early on, but what was most convincing
was that day in December of 1909 when I met Alma Winkler, then
in her eighties. We spent an afternoon together over cakes and tea
talking of life at Kingdom Farm."

Emma Goldman, *My Life*, p. 203

He might have made a revolution—
or something—rise radiant out of Kansas—
absurd as that sounds, but more believable,
I'd think, than the Paradise he expected
to lift, blossom, and sway in the grains' gold acres.
How could so wise a man have come
to such . . . what? not conclusions—
and *visions* is so . . . cloudy a word
but for the kind you'd expect him to have:
why he'd read Engels as early as Marx had!
and he called on armies to rescue children,
to attack factories and do . . . God knows what:
flame the wheel till angels, their fire-blades drawn,
can mend the axle's inner core,
whatever all that could have meant—
something about justice, I'd guess, but that's no way
to organize an army. He was more poetry
than insurrection. But the way he netted people to him!
he could have made those shattering states
correct themselves, hold, and shine
had he not been so *touched*—so sprung
by irrelevancies—the idea of a great harvesting god,
an overalled and farming Christ driving
a hundred Hoadeites and all Kansas
back through the barred gate and into Eden—
lunacy, sheer lunacy, of course. But what I'd give

to have sat with him there at the long table
and sipped the Kingdom cider
looking out over the bright and bending fields.

XVIII: The Last Survivor

"*Mary Wentzel Woodard, 93, of Chicago spent the first ten years of
her life at Kingdom Farm, Kansas, the socialistic religious community
which was established by reformer William Hoade in 1844 and flour-
ished for over a decade. She is the last surviving Hoadeite and. . . ."*

from "Kansas Celebrates 80th
Anniversary of Statehood," *Life,*
April 5, 1941

She was too old to remember much,
thought she remembered Hoade, the power
of his voice and word, his giving her a pear
once as she sat on her porch—not likely,
and certainly not his preaching; she was
too young—said the Farm
finally went broke after Hoade killed a man:
memory's old plates etched and effaced and etched again
and again—till so crosshatched and shadowed out
details blur into details, days into days
as we'd wish them lived, a life of reasoned words
at all the proper moments uttered. But her childhood did blaze
again and again when she spoke of taste or smell
or the color of what never quite turned Paradise:
the red flare-fall of elm and oak; or new-mown fields
bailed and lofted up, seizing whole barns with scents sweeter,
said Hoade, than Hiram's cedared palace and all glittering Tyre;
or the pungent difficulty of the cheese shed,
the slow fall of milk-white brine from linen bags
rank as the warm, heaped tubs of slaughter time,

but cheese white as Momma's aprons every morning,
cheese better than all the food of the rest of her life;
a fine dust that powdered the blackberries
she gathered for the breakfasts of Elders,
the humming wasps that nested there
and waiting to sting in the brambled thorn;
and everything bathed in light;
and on and on until you knew, till you were sure
memory's reels ran true, knew you, too, heard
his voice and tasted the pear, knew age drives
memory Heavenward in spite of error
and that it edits, that it corrects the past
into Paradise.

Shitheads

Their hardiness comes without effort,
as easily as salvation swarms
out of men who've heard their names
cried from clouds. But it's the urgency
of their need one most notices, how
from their furious grips and wide, white smiles
their eyes leech to yours, and their voices,
warm and as smeared with vibrato as a preacher's,
swoop over you like a fumbling lover,
and you are mauled by their appetites,
their measured dreams and confessions,
hopes shaped from the architecture of excess.

These men know where they are going,
and they insist their futures upon you, beg you
to smile back in mirrored vacancy the same smile
that sits on their faces, clean and neat as their rectums.
And knowing the paving will soon turn
to gold and their speed will increase again and again,
knowing it's all close enough to smell,
they scramble for the things they will need:
carphone, Rolex, deodorant. They buy up the secrets
of success: a Masonic handshake, a Rotarian luncheon,
the arcana of wine or futures, the vocabulary of ease;
and as they rise, they slough off the roles they've outgrown
like old skins or embarrassments. There's no goal
but ascension. And they know that God's floating eye
on the backs of dollars looks down on their work,
approves and blesses them.

Sometimes if you are lucky, you can glimpse them
as they pass, can hear their voices
trailing like crepe streamers.
But at such swarming speeds they're pitched too high
to catch; are indistinct as pond spawn;
are like the cold rushing syllables I hear
each winter mazing the webbed pockets of my walls.

Reflections on the Progress of the Western Intellectual Tradition from Thales to Crick and Watson

1. The Mystery

My hands have held
apples, and my fingers
slipped the pure curve
of pears as they have
slipped through lace
and linen to circuit
the curves of love
with no thought of why,
with no thought
of lust's cool compass
or the blind geometries
of desire.

2. The Comedy

If thinking does existence prove,
I must beware of crowds and eyes;
for if I think too long on love,
private proofs materialize.

3. The Tragedy

We dream of spiraling spells
down the twined helices of the heart.
But the heart is out of plumb. Fine tools
cannot survey its slant—nor even art
align what's long lain at the bestial point.

Hunting for a New Chairman;
Thinking about Giotto

Even the old ones puffed with uric acid
and swollen feet attempt a briskness
now that joy comets down close. They spin
like bits of dirt and lint tumbling in the sunlight
through these corridors of hope and dream.
They speak and smile again, and though it's eight
do not smell of last night's ease. No bourbon's needed
to whiskey dreams these waiting weeks,
for they're drunk on new space, a place
where files bright as this year's dimes
bulge with the secrets that have obsessed whole years:
why Professor X resigned or what the cheerleader
really said about Professor Y and on and on.
Their tongues begin to taste again and wander the room
that smells of new shoe leather and smaller mortgages,
a room spinning as securely as a chairman's clock
ticking the fat, tenured years into gentle sloth.
They dream the hopes of mazed rats,
and all joy rests in the right turn, the move
that leads to cheese and whole semesters of sleep,
to things that are for them like starlight
and the music of spinning moons, girls in gossamer
so thin no guessing's necessary, or a chapel
in Padua, for example, where stars once fell
to a man's moving hand, where wonders began.

Professional Dreams

FOR DENISE BETHEL

1.

As formless as the tissues
they seek, the dreams of oncologists
spread into their sleep, swarm
and swirl in the dark. A firm hand
reaches out to them
but turns before it meets theirs
to the texture of lung or brain,
bruised, purpled, transforming
to shapes as large as a child or car.
And it takes their hand, their arm
like things from the late shows.
But they are dumb and lack
their little knives or the agile mind
of a Price, a Cushing, some nemesis
of monsters, and soon
it is all over them.

2.

She dreams of pencils and steno pads,
of her legs crossed in a short skirt,
the pencil going back and forth
from pad to her lips as Mr. Bigboss
dictates the perfect orders of her life.
In her dreams the movies never lied,
never told her that steno pads
and dictaphones were no more
or that tapes and computers were as close

as she would ever come to Mr. Bigboss,
who will never look into her eyes
at a certain point, on an ordinary word,
like *sincerely*, for example, and it would be like
stars oblivious to physics, caste, and fortune,
breaking from their galaxies
and rushing toward each other,
their planets and responsibilities
hurtling outward toward oblivion,
and joy joy joy everywhere in her life.

3.

They are all girls and sixteen summers grown,
all naked, their nipples out
like the erasers on their No. 2's,
their textbooks and minds all open
and waiting for the most wonderful lecture
of their sixteen years. And he begins,
though he cannot remember what he said,
but formulas flow from him. His hands
are like lightning as they chalk
the equations of wonder to the blackboard,
and the girls know they witness miracle.
Though they are still taking notes,
their desks have somehow vanished
and he can see that their legs
have opened and their pencils are furious
in the transcription of wonder
and he knows that they will be thankful,
appreciative, for the rest of their lives,
that they will never forget him
or the beautiful algebra of his dreams.

4.

In all his years he has never
spoken like this before.
His voice is deeper, more
like flowing gold than voice,
the quavers like rainbows, wide
as his arms outstretched embrace
as scripture falls from his lips
like perfect pearls before jewelers.
And it is miracle. And they all hear.
Their sins fall away; their lives
change as they turn their backs
on whores and cards, tobacco, beer,
and the words that drive God mad.
And he sees the walls of his church
fall away and their clothes fall away
and they are naked but without shame
and trees are filled with fruit
and monkeys are asleep in the arms of lions.
And the deepest voice he has ever heard
says to him *Thank you; you **have** done well.*

5.

She is after him, and he knows it.
The blue light spins over the top
and the siren cries *I'm going to catch you.*
Her partner is no longer with her
but she needs no one as her car turns
into the alley and she sees him,
the serial rapist of little girls,
the beast they'd sought for years.
He is up against the bricks
with no where to go, crouched and crying,

begging for the mercy he lacked.
And she is out of her car, advancing.
And oh how he cries when he sees
high in her hand a razor blade
big as a manila envelope.
And she advances, advances
with sure and surgical precision.

6.

The lepidopterist is where
no lepidopterist has ever been.
It is a lost valley, probably in Tibet,
and it is all aflutter
with great green lunas
and marsh satyrs, phaetons
bigger than nets, and *Basilarchia*
bluer than any waking blue;
Lycaena and *Kricogonia*
but iridescent as opal;
Neonympha, Epidemia,
Heliconius, and *Polygonia*
big and soft
as cats and unafraid
and purring like cats
when they are petted.
They all love being petted
having never before encountered
a lepidopterist or a hand.
And all are to be named
for nothing like them has been seen.
And the perfect poem of nomenclature
goes on and on till morning breaks
to spoil the dreamer's pure Adamic joy.

Dreams of Standing

The retarded boy
thumbed the art book
and twisted his head
with the resolve
of a bug's head twisting
toward food, and stared
as if his eyes were
lidless bulges. Then
he spread his legs there
on the floor of the bookshop
where the breasts,
the uncluttered pubis, the dense
wood, the apples, the thick coils—
soft, scaleless,
like a fat woman's arm
widening in its heavy rise—
shimmered him. And it was like
riding, like the grinding spin
of his great tricycle's wheels,
that slight pressure at his anus,
his legs firing like shouts
to piston the miles, working
as they worked in dreams of standing
near them, their faces just
beginning to pimple, sullen,
pouting at their virginity,
and smelling of ripenings:
crusted cheeses, clean laundry
flapping in the bright cold.
And the boy would sweat
in those dreams like these

sweated him now. But in bed
and in the thickness of his dream
he could focus his tongue to twist
his eyes awake and rise and ease the dream,
but here on the floor of the bookshop,
unfocused, alone with Eve
and awake, his lips drying,
beginning to crust and glisten
like snailwork, there was
no salvaging, no salvaging
of himself at all.

Locomotion and Starlight

The light was cool as it drifted
down into my grandmother's garden,
into the stalks of corn,
the blades and pods of garlic.
Under such stars old men
thinking only of pensions and biscuits,
the cinders they've survived,
have slumped over, gone out like wet fusees;
firemen have lost count of coal
and huge wheels have slowed;
smiling call boys
punctual with dispatches
and the rousing of brakemen
have dreamed the dreams
of a drunk at the switch.
Though my grandmother said,
Certain signs are good for crops.
And the man next door who used to fire
but now made medicine said,
The garlic's ready to be ground.
And a call boy said, *In a month*
I'll be switching. And the light frolicked
through my grandmother's dark pantry,
fingered the jars of salves and preserves,
invaded the suppers of her lodge,
climbed the trellises, hammered hydrangeas,
and strutted to the turkey
as if it were a shape, a thing, an invited guest.

Babies on the Beach

To call their presence incongruity
is to say nothing about them, nothing
about them as a unit, plump and naked,
ignorant of cadence, moving like clouds
across the sand, their brows bent
in obvious and resigned anger at the tasks
before them, at the immensities presented
by beach and sun, by sand and drifts
of uncountable shells split from their pairs,
smaller than their fingertips, anonymous
and unnameable even had they desire
and all of time to sit and choose them names,
shells clean as the sea leaves the long-wrecked.
But what of their weapons? The claws
of washed out crabs, the blade shards of conch,
drift wood and weed for rope. But most
their tiny wills which melt and cast the lead,
cast casing for what the will has mined.
But what is that will, and why is it set
among metals, nitre, and sulphur?
And what is it determined in the presence
of those unnavigable immensities to chart?
Is it set against the fathers and mothers
fled from the beach, for weeks at least now gone,
gone long enough for them to perceive
desertion and then community, and later to arm,
to weld their wills to a single urge?

Large birds circle the shore; big fish
eye the land; these babies can't go on for long.
Wrath's brittle diet fragiles the freshest bone,
and soon in a great swooping and lunging
they will all be taken like tiny wrecks,
up and out and back again, one
with the immense, the anonymous, the clean.

Elegy for B. Kliban, Artist, Being a Meditation with Subverted Meaning on the Patron Saint of Crullers

I often ask myself,
"Now just who was
this Patron Saint of Crullers?
And was his mission pure?
Did he come to his tasks
through love?
Through hope?
Or was it mere desire:
a will to whirl the dough
and spin the shapes,
to twirl the crullers into curls
and drop them in the boiling oil,
the need to make the dough obey
and bow in crullered furls,
a lust to watch the crullers rise,
to puff and float upon the oil,
the wish to have all Holland's hope
puff out and fatten like the dough,
a wish to pile them high
and sail them forth
to set before those boys and girls
whose bleeding, splintered feet
called out for leather shoes and rest,
a rest with curds and cream,
and crullers blest?
But were *this* so
was not that saint
no more than some foul cook,
a thing of grease and flour,
of constant plots,

a thing to trap the heart
of every child and make him think
that even crullers have their saint?"
To make him never ask,
"Then who's the saint of sugar cane?
And did his sweat not fall
from brow and face and from his arms
in small, in sweet and geometric forms?"

Star Washer

He could wash the stars right out of your eyes
or put them back, bring down Babel
with a look, or rear the rim of Jericho
up from all its busted brick.

He turned the swaying garlic into wands,
and made a mud-smeared Eve forget her fear,
made her lift and hold her fanged,
uncoiled, her cold and honeyed nightmare.

He knew what turned from uncertain
into blue and how feet could fall
to strong love where hummingbirds
are strung to charm the spirit's spark.

Within the compass of his focused eye,
star-strewn ways zodiaced into shapes
to shape their heaven-bodies new
and fill the famine-dark in firefly light.

The Last Model

A Postscript: In February of 1977 the last surviving von Gloeden model died at Taormina. He was 87 years old.

Charles Leslie in *Wilhelm von Gloeden, Photographer*

I was lovely then—fourteen I think.
I'd never had a girl, never seen a gold coin,
knew nothing of gentlemen's ways.
In those days girls stayed too close
to mothers and prayer books—
not like today. And what would a fisherman know
of gold or fine manners? But I learned.

I would go up to his studio,
and *il Barone* would pour me wine,
sweet, cold wine from Germany. And—
after a glass or so, he'd take off my clothes.
I let him, you understand, because he was kind,
and generous. My wife often asked
if I had let him love me.
I'd tell her not to be so foolish.

He like to pose me beside ruined columns
and wrap vine leaves in my hair—
as if I were some boy god, he'd say.
His pictures made me beautiful; I remember that,
though I haven't seen one in fifty years.
He gave me a few, but my wife found them once.
She said they were only fit to start fires.
But I *was* beautiful. *Homeric*—
that was the word he used. My wife said
he told her brothers and cousins the same,
but she lied about everything.

He was good to me, took me on walks,
gave me coins and told me I was beautiful.
Though he's been dead for years,
I wish I could see him again,
walk together and drink cold wine.
I'd ask him if he still recognized me.
My face is not really so wrinkled, you know.
And we'd talk of the old days
when he called me his Ganymede.
I think Ganymede was a god, wasn't he?

Odysseys of Desire and Thoughts of Cavafy

When you looked at him
and thought you saw
your look returned,
hope and lust wed again
to make you think
you weren't so old,
and make you think
love's gifts might lie
as close and willing
as your hand,
that words might come
as easy now as Grecian smiles at rest
on Grecian lips, on God-faced boys
bearing wine in lotus blend, warm bread
and the dense and golden-clovered comb.

But what are love's options
when more than half your life is done:
the chance or charm of luck;
or drachmas stacked on table tops?

Love's never a certainty
when youth has fled,
less sure than even
in those worst of days
when tossed on beds of grief,
unable to rise or act,
you waited to hear *his* voice
call out your name—
when hope still had its chance.

Silage

The way she wore sweaters
and brushed her hair
made all the boys wish
she'd play strip poker
and dance like the woman
who came to the fair each fall
and undid those fresh boys
still dreaming of damp middle fingers
and barns filled with hay and dollars,
undid their stiff fathers
away from wives and tired
of thick-boned women who smelled
like bacon and sweat, undid
their thick mothers tired of prized cakes
and quilts, of jars of perfect jam, of "yes,"
and undid their wheezing grandfathers
fogged over by angina and age,
old men grinning as the past
stirred again in their laps.

Jesus, the things she did to those boys
when she wore sweaters and did her hair like that!
When they slept, they thought of her
naked and limp, her muscles turned
to mud, thought of themselves over her
giggling like their grandfathers;
thought of rich barns and kitchens,
the denseness of corn,
thick acres with ears bursting open
spilling dimes into their pockets;
thought of crops they'd harvest
as easily as girls. And breasts

and thighs, damp deep triangles of hair,
bright pails of cream, and hooves
thick with glue, whole boxcars
of marbled meat, and fat as white
as milk flowed in and out of their sleep
blending and rising
like the rank, rich silage
they could always smell,
that they could always taste
on the backs of their teeth.

The Myths of Meanness

And then he chewed her whole breast off,
or so my grandmother told me
and whispered to me of meanness
as she recounted dark details
that she and certain frightened friends
alone knew all about, but which,
of course, and wisely so, were hushed,
for they dared not and would not had they dared
declare to widows and virgins
the details of meanness.
And she said, *there's a lot*
of meanness going around now.
And I told her that I did not believe
her story, that I'd heard the same story
before and in other places and that
if she could remember, she too
would recall it. It was the same,
except that it was always told,
depending on where it was told,
about a Black or Indian or Chinaman.

And I thought of all the myths of meanness:
those gleaming silver hooks
left dangling from car doors
when cars in just the lucky nick
pulled away from down the petting lanes;
or the tiny black widows burrowed in
those stiff, unwashed, and daily sprayed bouffants,
black widows with hourglasses as red
as what those girls had planned to give
for beer, for football boys, and even love
later that special night,

hourglasses counting away
all the pretty prom queens' final dances;
or finally, wrapped in a shimmer of evil,
the crying girl who begs a ride
from beside some bashed car and what was once
her sweet-tongued boy,
only at her sad father's door to leave
and leave a sad father weeping
over a twenty-year-dead girl
and leave the countless and perplexed drivers
dark roads to follow home.

It was a white man that did it,
she quickly said, sure now
she had a new story
and that the meanness was confirmed.

And all the old women
amid their rows of beets,
their fear of cheese, their furious sewing,
worried over the final days.

Bees

In my father's catalpa
deep in dead limbs
was the tiny growl of bees.
Saps had stilled and grown silent;
only the humming of bees
remained to rise
through the branches
where once green and freshness rose.
Now droned-songs alone
pushed from moldy hollows,
small siroccos
stirred by the swinging
of rusty wings.

I have seen the greed of bees
hanging on small fuzzed feet
as dense puffs of pollen
or heavy, heavy globes of nectar
pulling the legs
until they were like plumb bobs
in that bright quiet of afternoon
when gathering is solitary
and children's eyes are closed
and their ears silent
to the drone and friction
of thighs.

My mother ordered
the hooded men
who came with their nets
and boxes of fresh comb
and fire to smoke the bees,

but they swarmed
and it was like blood hovering in the air
and the tree was burned.
And I still remember the final spindles of smoke
and my father beside me
running his fingers through his ashen hair.

Remembering My Father Riding

Though I was still a child,
I remember him (already too old
for such showings off) wobbling,
smiling, waving from the bike
as he circled the grape arbor
and rode between the tomatoes and peas,
smiling and waving, and me
crying, "Daddy, Daddy, stop."
I could see his feet slipping,
the wobbling bike going down,
and him falling into the garden,
into the tomatoes, their stakes
hitting his face, his glasses shattering,
could see him lying still,
the bicycle wheels still turning,
and dust rising and glistening in the sun.
And I called and called to him,
but he just kept riding,
kept circling the arbor
through the tomatoes and peas,
kept circling and smiling,
circling and circling the garden,
and smiling and waving
and smiling and waving.

For My Father

I'd wheel him strapped to his chair
down the long ramps and out
into the shade of the catalpas
so we could watch them fire the bees,
drive them from the walls of the house
where yearly they'd hive and honey.
And soon a smoke of kerosene
and burnt sugar would drift up
to the trees with the rising swarm.
And the peeled-back boards would reveal
deserted webs, matted and thick as dreams,
and broken bits of comb,
the wild black honey oozing.

I still sometimes dream of him,
of open windows and the long, warm springs,
the smell of grass and wild onion,
the noise of mowers at dusk
and the sway of the great snowball bushes
blooming up and down the length of Second Street,
iron fences and terraced yards
and jonquils that seemed to race April
just to frame our lawn,
and my father beside me,
erect and unbound.

Thinking of My Mother

She lived into her death
and was gone before her dying.
All but her breath
wrecked years before.
Her brain's once lively pages
crumpled into tight wads,
grew hard as rock. Voice, eyes,
teeth, bladder, bowels—
all wrecked in the frail bag
of flesh that once contained
generosity beyond measure.

I am glad, though, it was she
who so long lay there not dying
instead of me. Each visit
broke tears or rage, then finally
nothing from me, nothing
but the desire to flee as I stood there
bending over her, talking
of weather and mail and relatives
as if her ears had not shut
and I had not tumbled from her memory,
as if I would not have rather been
anywhere else.

Had she watched over such ruin
of a thing once me, her only child,

her whole history
would have slipped into disaster,
every breath into regret.

I know this, having my son
here beside me, having learned
love's lessons in her generous abundance.

Snapshots from the Fifties

How ugly we were back then,
all of us. Look at her fur,
her glasses, the veils
and gloves. And his hat,
like some old fart's,
and the elbow patches, and me
in a fancy cowboy shirt,
two front teeth out, smiling.

God! Could that have been us?
The woman who read me poems
and played the piano daily.
The man who taught me kindness
and handed me the heroes
I still hold. The boy
who would turn into me?

Sometimes on television now
I watch those days re-run
and remember how we all laughed
and enjoyed the obvious.

She would watch Welk weekly,
charmed at how Florian would smile
and smile as he worked his accordion
in and out, curious—weekly curious—
whether the bellows' motion
or if those bubbling tunes alone
tickled him into the smiles he wore.
She was saddened when Aladdin
left and no violinist was ever

so gypsy or so good again.
She who played for me and read?

And why did he, as far as we were
from water, buy a speed boat,
join the Shrine, organize
that awful scout troop?
He—who loved Gompers, Debs, and Ché?

What hold did those days have
on hearts like theirs? And what
might Dafydd look back to mock
that now moves me—powerfully
as thoughts of speed,
of water shimmering to diamonds
in the sun and bounding prow,
or sound glittering like gold Tokay
spilling from sultry casks,
spilling into my mother's kitchen,
spilling out all Romany, Araby, and Champagne.

Remembering a Young Poet
I'd Known in College

His going seemed less sad
than that there was so little to mourn
after he'd gone. It was all too artificial
for serious tears—or to matter;
deaths like those don't,
not in the run of things.
He was all parody, myth-mad and anxious to nova,
to flame out young, to beat Berryman by thirty years
and then edge out the whole singing suicide team.
So he blew holes in his chest.
And he and all possibility evaporated, burned off
like morning fog, to mingle
with the fates of other lonesome children:
the fat boy who locked himself in the refrigerator
when his parents said no more cake;
the girl who jammed scissors in her unkissed breasts
because her tv idol liked to get drunk
and drive fast, could now never answer her letters
or desire; and child after fragile child.
So he, too, made his graceless gestures,
large center stage struts with great waving
of the arms and profiling of the head,
him playing Jack Oakie playing Mussolini,
but to an empty house
and years too soon, years before some grace
might have mantled down to laurel or foil
or merely dignify a tired and tawdry plot
that never worked.
There was no tragedy left, not at that point,
not even the waste; it had set in long before,

back when the good old boys
dead-ended him with praise and he was made to think
he could pick and choose the mask desire would wear.
But I do remember a summer night though
when I could have wept for him,
when we listened to Puccini
over and over till dawn
and drank mavrodaphne, warm and sweet
as his breath,
and he held me,
held me with all the secrets
he would soon have
under his perfect control.

Elegiac Stanza on a Photograph
of Ethel Rosenberg in Her Kitchen

It sits on top my desk, but it is faced
So that the sun will not cause it to fade:
The photographs we save are like the taste
Of honey on a sharpened razor blade.

Elegy

It has already been observed that being an American
is difficult. I reobserve, renote the fact: it is
difficult. And I don't know what to do about it.
I think it has been this way for some time now,
a long time in fact, though the last ten years
have seemed, how shall I put it, "memorably difficult"?
And these last few days? They have been very hard.
It's as if blood had dried on me, and when I move,
it flakes and falls and drops around me.
Flakes are at my feet. And I despair. I say things like
"It's not my fault; please don't blame me," or "I'm
nobody." To no avail. Excuses are useless.
Salvador Allende was murdered in Santiago, Chile,
two days ago. Excuses are useless. "I'm nobody."
Four U.S. battleships were positioned
off Chile's coast. Excuses are useless. Flakes
drop round me. I think they're shaping into words.
I know what they are spelling. I apologize.
"But you've got to understand I'm nobody." I lie
and say I'm from Canada. Excuses are useless.
Salvador Allende was murdered in Santiago, Chile,
and I despair. The White House has still made no
comment. Excuses are useless. I reobserve, renote,
and despair. To no avail. "And what if I were
an American; what could I do? I'm nobody.
I'm not the President." Excuses are useless.
"Not guilty, not guilty," I insist. To no avail.
Salvador Allende was murdered in Santiago, Chile,
and I despair. Excuses are useless. Allende is dead.
I despair. To no avail. Allende is dead. It is difficult.

Elegy in September

FOR MAO

Though golden carp still flash and swim
and wheat is sickled and brought down,
though plums are still to prune and trim,
the central man is gone.

Elegiac Ode

Stop and lament over the grave of Kroisos, whom
furious Aries destroyed one day as he fought in the
front ranks.

inscription on a kouros figure,
circa 520 B.C., in the National
Archeological Museum, Athens

He stands and smiles a smile to stun our sight.
His Attic lips reveal antiquity's disdain
    For all the centuries to come, the blight
Of brutish air, a blighted future's trashed terrain.

Could Delphic voices turn and laurel his lips again to song,
    I'd have them chorus on and on.

But now it is for Kroisos I lament,
Whose smile of certain logic Aries kissed one day,
    Though still his supple beauty is unspent
As when his lips were poised in pure tranquility.

Could classic song return and animate his scattered dust,
    We'd pray him back from Aries' lust.

Excess has driven its barbaric weight
Through near a million days since Kroisos stepped from stone.
    Could gold and Grecian mean now tolerate
the measures of intemperate time, an age of bone?

Could Kroisos stand and rise to song, his lips would still remain
    Fixed in perpetual disdain.

The Bathers

FOR JUSTIN CALDWELL

the heart is out of plumb

What drives the eyes, drives them back
again and again? Is it merely so much flesh
and revelation, the nakedness alone?
No, not even theirs, innocent and easy as it is,
though that alone could compel the coolest eye,
compel it to a honed distraction—or to linger.
Attraction?—yes, but that's always inexplicable
and roused effortlessly, it seems, lifts
like miracles
in uncontrolled mystery from face
to certain face and is not particular to them;
nor even desire—oh, there is desire, of course,
but not just for limbs and lips,
those curves of compulsion, their costly lines,
but for the scene itself, for it to be
and be and be, for all those clear years
before the century's turn, for wide light
and water, the ease of them together,
their agile geometry
and the consolation of a settled world,
summer days and shimmering pools
where innocence itself once bathed
in embracing lengths of providing light.

i. Seurat, *Une Baignade*

I was on the other bank
and couldn't hear him,
but I think he was saying,
"Come over here."
I waved back at him.
He could see it was too far,
at least for me to swim,
and we didn't have a boat.
Mama wouldn't have let me
anyway. She'd just opened
our picnic basket and taken out
a roasted chicken and fat spears
of cool, white asparagus.
And he could see she'd put a cloth
on the grass and Papa was waiting.
Maybe he was a better swimmer than I,
and he and his brother would swim over later.
I could see that my sister noticed his brother,
was watching me, was also hoping.
After lunch Papa would fall asleep
and Mama would sit and watch boats,
watch the way light jeweled the water,
and the boy and I would play sailboats.
My sister and his brother would stroll.
She was always strolling with boys.
I once told her she would stroll her life away
if she wasn't careful. But she told me
I was stupid and childish, that her days
were made for strolling, that even summer
would stroll away and leave you
if you didn't go with it.

ii. Bazille, *Scène d'Eté*

I stood there against the tree waiting
for him to turn toward me,
but the two boys wrestling on the grass
were his eyes' only concern.
Perhaps they'd tire in the bright heat,
and he'd tire of watching, would turn
and talk to me, and we'd bicycle back
together, and I'd invite him to my room
and we'd have some wine and pears,
would talk of teachers or books or maybe girls
and the villages we came from,
our mothers' kitchens
and how they smelled in the mornings
and the abundant smell of evening—
Papa's tobacco and hay still stuck to his shoes
and sweat woven into his shirt like a design—
and we'd talk till morning
or till we fell asleep
together to dream of each other,
dream of swimming,
all summer long swimming
silently, slowly, together,
soundless, gliding
deftly as dolphins
through perpetual pools
of shimmering summer.

iii. Cezanne, *Baigneurs*

We'd been on maneuvers and were camped down the road.
It was Marc and Gilles who first found it.
They came back wet and laughing,

and someone said let's all go
and off we headed, Gilles leading.
He was like things you saw in the Louvre,
things dug out of Italian volcanoes
and that old Popes kept in their bedrooms—
but he was more than looks—
generous and kind and all that. But Marc!
Who knew what Gilles saw in him!
Marc had a girl back in his village,
kept her picture, showed everyone.
He'd return to her some day. Even Gilles
must have known that. But who knows
what anyone sees in anyone; the heart
is an odd clock, I always say.
I told him Marc was no good,
would hurt him worse than any girl, but he just smiled
and told me what good friends we were. Like that day.
That day! That pond! Heaven!
I've remembered it for years.
We were like children again—
swimming, laughing—but what I most remember
is how he just stood there, holding a towel,
looking off, maybe at the trees or the sky,
and he was beautiful. But that wasn't what I was thinking;
I wasn't envying Marc. He was beautiful, but it was more
than that. He looked—I know this sounds foolish—
blessed, like a Bible story—
like something about King David maybe,
but not one I remembered, like some picture
of one that might have been—a figure
on one of those parable cards the nuns used to give us
for right answers—or when we were good—
or knew the things to say.

But this is all gone today.
The last innocence fell away
in the trenches. The last Jonathan,
bright as some forgotten parable
and wooing our perplexed desire,
said goodbye somewhere in Belgium.
The ponds of perpetual summer dried up,
or were blasted.
And love has turned so commonplace
that couples now
need no strolls to rouse their blood.
We've solved the heart's arithmetic
but learned to fear its mythic sums:
the magic lies, the bonding hold.

And so, those crackled boys and peeling girls
look out at our poor luck,
stretch out their hands to ours.
And though we will not touch
or ever be so free again,
we can recall their generous gestures
and turn from the fluxions of stars
and chromosomes, blind, denying
our bitter solutions, denying
our hungering, bestial hearts.

Flowers for Robert Mapplethorpe

i

Near the Pantheon
a boy whose shoulder shows
the purple of desire,
whose muscled chest
is brown as dying callas,
offers the tourists flowers
and expensive chestnuts
out of season.

His jeans are as tight
as the unblossomed peonies
I think of buying. I ask him
how long before they open.
"Tomorrow," he lies. Still
I take bundles back
and chestnuts, too. Tonight
he and his leathered
bully-boy will think of me
when they buy wine and vaseline,
will think I am waiting
tomorrow's hard buds to open
as I sleep, will think
I'll awaken in a kind of tourist's rage
with what the night has made.

ii

There are always flowers left
on the grave of John Keats.
Neat school boys in blazers

leave the roses they bought
on the Spanish Steps. And they
go home to England intending
to think, henceforth,
on beauty alone, and always
tell the truth. Thick ladies
in suits come to lay violets
there. They hand new cameras
to strangers who blur them
but save for a fall's coming class
some proof of love, some sketching
of why their eyes glaze so
when they speak of him, glaze
like sex or preaching,
to prove a love
they've forced for years indifferent teens
to learn like prayers.
     Some will recall
an urn, a bird, a silent peak,
a blurred, bending figure placing violets
once when they were young, their skin
quick as matches, when they hated
school and Keats and anything that held
the eyes, the tongue, the hands
from love's circuit, those gaudy explorations
older, richer than the oldest poems.

iii

Wheat and poppies bloom
along the Appian Way.
Bees have built
into the broken walls,
and honey slips down

the bricks.
A motor cycle passes.
The sound is mean as bees,
angry as a hundred hives.
The boy in rear holds
the hips of his friend
tightly, and they both are
laughing as if the comb of the world
was dense, was full, was theirs.

iv

Crossing the Ponte San' Angelo,
I see a page ripped from a magazine.
A penis is poised for entry
from behind. A long-haired girl
looks over her shoulder and speaks.
In a balloon over her head the words
are written out. She says, "Stick it in."
Bernini's statues look down.
Hadrian's tomb rises in front.
A man carrying roses and bread
passes me, also notices the page.
"There's nothing you'd want there,"
he says. He is younger than I,
looks neither prude nor lunatic,
but is wrong. Had I enough Italian,
I'd tell him No, that I want
the mean words of their rough love,
that I would take them and make silent
as the rise of bread their copulation,
that I would press them like roses
or fold them like a friend's handkerchief
stiffened with the crust of need.

Coda

The bruised boy found leather
for his labor, and the bikers
alone where poppies bloom
saw honey break from a wall.

But those leaden virgins in love with Keats,
the boy bringing home bread and roses
only found ritual at the petals' lips—and shadows,
the shades of lusts embraced in sleep alone.

The Mysteries: Elegy at Century's Close

IN MEMORY OF FREDDIE MERCURY

1. The Symbol

Moments before you might notice the glove,
her face would hold your gaze until
her nipples radiant beneath the lace
took your eyes in a dazzling of copper,
and in a kind of shame at the discovery,
the theft, your eyes would drop to the white glove
held as she might hold some animal, limp,
drugged, and you would stare at the folded glove
white and wounded, but radiant in glories
of abundance, soft at the prism's thrill
where colors in vibrating conjunction
separate to fall into cold order.
And it demanded ecstasy, magic,
demanded all philosophy's closure
and the slow aphrodisia of praise,
a praise whole thrusting days were required
to raise. And then the glove slipped from her hand.

You thought to pick up the glove, to return
to her hand this thing that out-thrilled her face
and all the soft wealth of her breasts,
but it was gone. And not until later
on the frozen pond did you see it
as tartan mufflers snapped the air
and skates knifed along ice as hard and grey
as winter's hanging sky. The air
itself seemed cast in grey, and snow began
to fleck the air and fall on skaters there

spinning in circles on the ice in grey
winter's perfect afternoon's cold cold air.
And on thick grey ice lay the glove burning
while oblivious boys skimmed past the balanced
girls a-twirl as snow scattered in their hair,
swift, silent, past the glowing glove aware
only of friction, and the pond's rapid return.

Near the old bakery, now a powdered ruin—
though the air still seemed to hold the odor
of seed cakes and high risen loaves—the glove
lay in a stubble of dry grass, lay there
like softest flesh in a cradle of hair,
like something of porcelain and pearl.
And around it stood a crowd of men
staring. And you, too, were there staring,
frightened someone might reach into the grass
and take the glove before you could say,
"I've long sought . . ."

2. The Offering

Oh, we've always known
where love's tent was pitched.
There are no surprises down there,
down in the warm and yeasty dark.
But in the face! No one had looked
into love's Janus'd frame before,
into the death-head smiling there
and seen the eyes milky with memory's loss
barely holding their socket's space
while the breath molded over
and the cheeks fell to the bones' frame.

That love has come to exact such tribute
fouls its history. And even mystery's realm
withers smaller still:

Heaven-striding stars shaping to flesh;
or the rapturing, plentied fields of grain;
light sickled down in the wheelings of ripe flame;
and wine poured from water; or elegance from gabble
have all bowed to fact.
                          Now carbon unveils
the mystery and electrons unmask the myth;
and even we are unraveled
at some swollen, erogenous *I*
where we squat and cringe
grunting and grabbing.

And love, too, is mocked,
for it was love that took them,
not easy passion, not the labyrinths of lust;

even if his name's unknown, his lips
and body's pressure forgotten, the taste
of sweat lost with other tastes and other times,
need, regardless of its geographies,
is still love's *other* name: distinct, clear,
and pure as a patronym.

3. The Oracle

See them, those fleet of foot wending their way
through the grove in cadenced footfall, moving
like figures in a frieze—bright robed Bacchae
or glistening athletes. Yet see these proving
by their motions that it's not ecstasy
they seek nor any Delphic mystery.

The bus-loads come because they've heard they should,
not for words once poured pure as spring water
from the laureled lips of Pythia. She stood
where now slouches a droning tour leader.
Cameras go off, snap the scene randomly,
frame it in thin rectangular memory.

The world's ruined center mirrors now the heart's:
no longer does Doric discipline define
or tolerance mold discourse or the arts
to question our measure and design.
No oracles rise in blessings to ease
these days, days only fit for elegies.

The Testament of the Saints:
Fragments from a Requiem for Ronald Firbank

*"Do you really believe now, Mrs. Tooke my dear, in de Apostolic
Succession? Can you look me in de eyes and say you do?" "I ha'n't
paid any heed lately to those chaps, Mrs. Yaj; I'm going on to
Habakkuk." "Dat is not de name now ob a man, Mrs. Tooke, to
observe a single wife, nor even a single sex. . . . No! Oh no; a man
wif a name like dat would have his needs!"*

from *Valmouth*

Requiem and Kyrie (Caspar del Bufalo)

St. Vincent Strambi said that St. Caspar
del Bufalo's preaching was "like a
spiritual earthquake."
*O lub de Lawd or be consumed
by de flambations an burnations ob de spirit.
Hallelujah, lujah, lujah.*

. . . . .

There were groves of olives and frequent miracles
about the monastery. The odor of lemons was often in the air
when St. Caspar prayed, and crowds of old profligates
smelling of garlic, grits, and profligacy, given over
to the depths of dissipation kneeled
speechless before him waiting for things to return.
*Hep 'um, Lawd; hep 'um; come on now, Lawd;
hep 'um anyway. They needs hep; they needs it bad.*

Sanctus (Ioannes Silvanus)

St. Ioannes Silvanus was denounced
for his hagiography. The old Pope said,
"He intemperate of tongue,
oddly notioned, and elliptical."

So the old Pope
put on the big gold hat
with the big bright ruby
and went out at twelve noon
to push St. Ioannes's statue
right into the Tiber,
down with the dirt and fishes.
But nobody could find it,
so some old cardinal told the Pope
they must have forgotten to make one.

"Maybe he no real saint.
I understands
be no accounts
of de miraculous acts
though he claim
to hab seen de germ
wif his naked,"
says the old Pope.

An apocryphal story relates
how he once told a stuttering boy
that Jesus was a wasp. St Odo said,
"Now dat's quite a story.
Who dis St. Sylva think he be?"

Agnus Dei (John Bosco)

Children attested to his miracles: *Day's de best.*
Savio to his hands: *Ummmm.* Bosco had hands
like a Southern girl's, creamy as hominy.
The Negroes were so envious: *We envious.*
They'd come in from the fields, hot and tired
from harvest, from loading the wagons with linguini,
and Old Pietro would take out his red bandanna,
wipe the sweat from his old black brow, and say,
"We jes lubs yo hands, Sig. Bosco. They are quite
aesthetically satisfying. Please preach to us now
and make many digital gestures." O his hands were lovely.
Madame Curie commissioned Rodin to turn them to bronze:
Makes me a statue now, please. Rilke elegized them
as angelic: *Day angelic.* And Richard Strauss
composed *The Hands of Bosco* in their praise:
Dis not de kind ob tone-poem I usually writes.

They were like the hands
of Southern girls
when they curved and moved
through Savio's curls.

Lux Aeterna (Dominic Savio)

When I died, John wept for me for hours
and the old slaves brought flowers
and told him the things they'd seen,
things unnatural and mean:
love, honey, and sweet milk gone sour.

But John saw love made larger, said,
"I have wandered within the compass,
an elect and measured arc,

and there divined the theorem
and grafted out the grace,
and saw the Christ aglow
in eyes of every child."

Confutatis (Agnes of Montepulciano)

When de Spring comes, first I thinks ob de crucifixion,
den I thinks ob de resurrection,
an den I thinks ob de . . .
An sometimes I dreams ob spiders spinnin me,
webbin me wif sin and bundlin me for a snack.
Dey dance on my . . . an' angelic choirs
ob . . . with . . . big as (oh my!) baseball bats
sings me to sleep like when I's a baby
back in de swamps ob Montepulciano.

Dies Irae (Odo of Cluny)

Odo wrote a poem about Christ's redemption.
I is de poet saint.
Odo is remembered for a sympathetic heart
and a lively sense of fun.
I good humored and hab de sympathetic heart
an dat's a good thing fo eve'body—saints imcluded—to hab.

Why I remembers de time dat Brother So and So . . .

. . . .

The terrible and beautiful arms of Christ came down
juvescent as the music of a gaggle of angels,
and Cluny was alive with light
and the Lord's most youthful figure.

Odo saw the Blond God in his straight white robe,
saw the radium filaments flaming against the edges.
But He did not move or dance the tarantella.
He only grew whiter and more blond and more radiant,
and Odo leaped out of the flesh,
dumbed and terrified.

Libera Me (Sebastian)

. . . . Ooooooh! . . . .

Thinking of Maria Theresa Broussard, a Pregnant Girl in My Freshman Class My First Semester in Louisiana

I am here at an end tip of things.
The Gulf curls in a few miles away,
and she comes to my office daily.
One is cautious of the weather here.
I'm told alligators are sleeping
in the mud only a few miles away.
I'm shown bottles of huge green pills
she takes for things I've forgotten.
Her mother and sisters are sad,
though the wisteria has been like
music this year, and the camellias
as tight as confectioners' roses.
She tells me about the boy and how he . . .
Since I've been here I've bought chances
on nine church-sponsored raffles sold me
in front of Kroger's on Saturdays.
Aphids are lush here, and I've learned
the proper proportions of poisons
and oilicides. And my wife's garden
has sprung from the wet dirt like babies.
In my office she shows me pictures
she's drawn: mice holding floppy flowers,
faceless children in antique bonnets.
She promises me a phoenix.
I smile and ask her how she's doing.
She twists her arms and shows me she is
double jointed. A friend is giving her
a C.B. radio. "It will help,"
she tells me. There are large green palms here,

and I think of their white hearts, but we
no longer import them from Brazil,
or so the man at Kroger's tells me.
"This is the end," he tells me. And so
I take them all. And she smiles at me
because it will help, and I ask her
what C.B. name she'll take for herself.
"Sophisticated Lady," she says.
She says, "Lots of people call me that."
"That's nice," I say. She brought me three bells
for my window, and I hung them there.
I've not asked what she'll name her child.
It will be born on her birthday,
she says. The Gulf curls in.
The wind has not moved the bells.

For a Friend Whose Son Committed Suicide

There aren't any words to help us live.
The days treat us like drunken husbands.
    Living demands we give
up everything we loved, and it hands
into our hands dirt, boxes of dirt,
    rooms of dirt, houses, whole houses
    of dirt. Though always at the start
we think we hear other promises.

    There are not any words to help us
when deaths and the other desertions
    come whacking and then leave us
lessened in their long divisions.
There is no act to perform against it.
    We weep until we stop.
    The quotient of loss is a wind
that blows memories away. It tastes like dirt.

Weights and Measures

That we can with so little effort
come to the limits of love,
to the limits of grief,
what we thought were the edges
of the map, where stars fall off
and fear swims, its sickening scales
glittering in the fire of its breath,
that we find it so easy, effortless
as disgust or boredom; that,
that is the weight
and measure of the world.

Oh, we weep until we stop, for sure.
But except for the death of a child,
it doesn't take long for the drying out,
the sobering, to feel the loneliness—
or like a fool—for sweet anger and lust
to worm their comfortable way home.

Time's passage is pure lotus,
and our forgetful eyes reanimate with ease;
thank God!—else we'd grind our hearts away with grief:
she leaves or he goes, and the heart comes apart;
inaction falls upon our days; earthquakes
and murder and holy war—but there's no suffering
like ours.
                    And then—a pair of lips'
certain set, the brows, the chest or breast—
and the clamps and joists,
all the tools and vises of the heart
unpack themselves and go back to work.
The world's diamond balance resets,

turns true again. And it—
and we—have found our proper spin
and comfortable gravity come home
to stay this time for sure.
Joy's idiot invasion—the re-tuning
of the spheres, new keys, new harmonies,
but the same monotonous song—advances:
the couldn't live without yous,
the I'll always be this or thats.

And the days grow summery, sultry,
weighted with sugars once more.
And we, singing like hungering,
musical bugs, rub our thises and thats together,
make the noise and smells of promise—
sustained in desire's amber, forever held
in our fierce and mutual cravings.

Seeing a Girl Who Looked like a Well-Known Child Actress Walking Toward San Tomé, the Church in Toledo Where El Greco's *Burial of the Count of Orgaz* Hangs

As dark and temptingly grown
and with the same eyes, the same
soft but near masculine head,
the same thick brows, and
with the same magical breasts
they both understood, she wandered
toward San Tomé and the *Burial of Orgaz.*
She paused at a cafe and the corduroyed boys
to see herself barely quiver in their stares,
barely come back
like a figure before a mirror
whose silver has slipped.
Too caught in themselves, their smokes and talk,
they hardly noticed the eyes, the head,
the brows, or even those breasts
they'd soon work days and spend days of work to taste.
And so she turned toward San Tomé, turned
toward the painting, and I watched her turn,
watched her move toward the doors,
saw her hand go out,
and I wanted to shout,
"Yes, yes, I understand."

But in moments she would be before it,
amid Japanese and nuns and tourists from Louisiana,
before it, before the dark face of the dead count,
before the dark and dying faces that surrounded him.
And she would see that though angels filled the air,

the bent body of Orgaz did not ascend,
that though Japanese and nuns and tourists from Louisiana
had come to a church, no hymns were on their lips,
no hands shook hallelujahs above their heads,
no tongues stuttered incomprehensibles of the New Jerusalem.
For here El Greco crowded out Christ, crowded him
with the dark, bent body of Orgaz and a grey dying
that pushed from under the doors, that ran
like soured honey down the alleys of Toledo, that rose
into the sky above Toledo and out and out and out.

And one who had seen the grey face of Orgaz
in his own, who'd taken his share of soured sweets
put his back to the painting
and moved in front of the girl
and stared at her breasts, stared
with such ripe and burgeoning prophecy
she turned from him and from Orgaz,
turned out the doors and back up the streets, back
to the cafe where again she looked
but only for the length of a laugh
and a quick toss of her long hair as she turned,
turned into the now clean, free and honeyed streets of Toledo.

Meditative Stanzas: On Stanley Spencer

FOR MORRI CREECH

I: Angelic Intercession (Spencer Speaking)

Could I command the planetary lyre,
lightning's chorus, the sky's timbrels and pipes,
I'd shake stars from the sky-roofs to choir
women, women, women to joyous heights.

And when they reached those peaks,
and downed their wings to rest,
they'd tell me what I seek
lies in their thighs, lies at their breasts.

II: Announcements

1: At the Moon's Pause

She stands watching it sickle into night,
her years' obscure umbrage, youth's bedlam glow,
and waits the clarifying fires of sight,
a centered orbit, a blazing halo.

But angels come with other plans
and spring the leg that leaps the womb
and bring youth back full-filled with pains:
a girl in silks and pretty plumes,
the hacking room, a salver's stain.

2: At the Moon's Rise

I bring you all the world's geometry
and set it in your womb and say, Lady,
this is what you shall bear, circle and square,
each angle, line, and plain, the shapes that wear
the shape of everything.
                              I'd rather have a child.
And husband! They'll all hate me and I'll be reviled;
I mean, how can I say that some fancy Angel
talking nonsense in circles made my belly swell?

Lady, not I who comes to spread your thighs
and slip your frame into the starred skies
of all the rest of history,
but *HE* who woos you in the cold glory
of numbers, woos you in pure paradigm,
the helixed equations of motion's rhyme,
laws that hold the spinning spirals
and knit your bones to star-cast fields.

And kings will bring you sweetest myrrh
and . . . *Oh stop, Angel! This has gone too far.*
Just tell me will my life get easier?

And laughter crackled in the air.

III: Baths

1. With Water

Having fed on God's wild honey
and lived so long with animals,

man's stink was what he'd wash away,
man's pride was what he'd cripple.

But he'd go headless in God's praise
and wind all history through
with naked girls who got their ways,
as naked girls can always do.

2. With Fire

Whipping with love's Galilean fever,
he ripped the temple markets down.

He knew the windy worth of high palaver
and preached his thought in deed alone.

When love and anger meet to right the world,
love's flesh is flayed and joy is rent.

But blessed wrath won't weep when it takes hold
for it makes man angelic instrument.

IV: Angelic Intercession (Spencer Speaking)

Her body is a galaxy
fit with moons, a milky way
which nightly I slip toward
to feel the rain of shooting stars.

Sphere-music's what I've heard,
the song of sexual lyres,
though others only see
an old and fearsome play.

Sacred Celebrations for the Moon's Beginning: Five Menarcheal Songs with Epigraphs from St. Simeon

1. Akathist for the Virgin

Light. Glory. Come, true light. Come light eternal. Light. Shining forth.

At the moon's beginning
she beheld in herself
the out-breaking of light,
beheld galaxies of love
spinning there
where she cradled
her future and her pain
and held generations
of unborn need
in the longing
her body had made,
in thorn, in nail,
in the world's blest
but bitter salvage,
risen now, spangling
from the virginal moon
and her immaculate
and hunting heart.

2. The Demon Brought Down on Breton Fields: Gauguin's *Vision after the Sermon* Redefined

Phos. Glory. Come reality beyond all words. Light. Shining forth.

St. Michael wrestles down the demon
and Breton fields incarnadine.
The demon neck is bent
beneath a hand of hammered rage;
the demon spine reports
above the gold wings' beat.

And Breton girls as they begin to bleed
will see this scene repair, repeat.

St. Michael wrestles their desire
on apple-bright and sermoned days,
but only women see
and only women hear
their broken demon's cry,
their broken demon's tear.

3. The Cheerleaders at St. Agatha's Middle School

Phos. Dhoxa. Come hidden mystery. Light. Shining forth.

Their days seem to whisper "Hurry, hurry;
you haven't much time."
But soon enough age slithers in
to force the rest of all their days
into the muscled hold of sex and death.

The boys stare where they hope
real breasts wait, even if not for them.
They watch the bells and tassels sway

at the tops of little boots,
and they cheer as they are led to cheer
when the girls leap
and spread their small legs in the air.
They cheer and cheer
for the sight of underwear,
the nylon veil,
the mystery's shield.

And soon on other nights
it's pulled away,
and their bodies thrill
and their voices rapture,
but nothing is explained;
no clouds unfold; no words unlock.
And no one knows anything, anything more
than they did before.

4. Communion at Glendalough

Phos. Dhoxa. Come light that knows no evening. Phos.
Shining forth.

She stood in front
of the waterfall
and posed herself
for the camera
the way her parents
had composed her
for Christ
and Christ's sake.
Her hands pressed
the lace of her dress
and straightened
a crooked St. Kevin

upon her chest
awaiting her
and her confessions'
budding wishes,
St. Kevin waiting
the last candle
she will burn
bright as new blood
this night
before sleep comes
brightly as all
the things
she will not know
that she has wished
and dreamed.

5. Akathist for Love: The Canonization of Cupid

Phos. Dhoxa. Come rejoicing without end. Phos. Epiphania.

The honeyed arm of Cupid held
his bow and steadied for the bees
alighted there, but they were stilled
and would not sting. When rising girls
awake to glow in Love's pure fire,
they coax and beg their sainted boy,
O bless the bees of man's desire,
distill the nectar of my joy.

The Honey of Hellas

In the gymnasts' grove thrives the shape
that shaped Athenian mastery,
not the self-sown, self-begotten olive
or the disciplined stone
but the living form made known
in gold proportions
beauty's cartographers alone
might compass out from flesh
to chart in pure geometry:
the buttock's chiseled curve,
the torso's even fall,
and love's enigma held
in gold and Doric balance.

★

And they were brought to their knees
the way no archaic form
had delivered them down,
driven like nothing the most Athenian hand
ever called from stone could drive,
for there in its presence
joy was juvenescent
as the figures of artifice.

And at those measures,
at their eyes' scansion
of the forms' pure promise,
they heard the high harmonies
of Pythagorean song.

★

Apollo and Dionysus,
hold me in your laureled groves
and let their precincts blend:
catch me
in the eunuch-pure
and marbled mathematics
of discipline,
in thought
freed from flesh and fragility,
in logic's harmonious oracle;
bind me in love out-spangling
time and the glittering isles,
out-spangling Delos and Naxos
and the honey-skinned gymnasts vaulting,
glistening there
where also drums and burns
the wine-raptured heart,
frenzied and driven
by no reason reason might devise.

And hold them, too,
in attic grace and attitude,
before their sweet arithmetic
begins to break
and buckle under age's weight,
and love and language
all begin to fail
and no more yield
the choral turn,
the kouros smile,
or youth's dumb honey.

ἡ ποιητική

I dream of perfect forms,
Of poems like Parthenons,
A frieze of fluid words
So cut in Attic odes
    Clarity blazes out to shine,
    And beauty—even in ruin.

Bare marble's windy frame
And gold Athene's ghost
Are all that now remain
To prove, or haunt, the loss
    Of intellect's purest moment
    And beauty's unadorned intent.

Those broken stones sing out
Brighter than any art
My pen or thought might craft
And make me try to carve
    The stone to find that shimmered sound,
    Those fluid folds of her marble gown.

Homage to Dafydd ap Gwilym

FOR DAFYDD GWILYM WOOD
charegl nwyf a chariad

The foam falls in fleeces big as fists
and snowflakes wander North Wales
like swarms of white bees.
I keep inside, can't sleep.
Even girls can't get me out.
Heaven makes us hermits and January is plagued,
as if God Himself had thrown down
the down of heaven's geese
till drifts billow over heather,
sway like swollen bellies, as if God wills
fine flour down and flour-lofted angels
cloaked in frost and quicksilver
lift the planks of heaven's loft
and dust down the thickets
of Wales like April's blossoms,
as if a load of chalk bows down the trees,
as if a coat of tallow, of cold grit had come,
and mail and dragon scales, a leaden coat
whose rude power makes us wait the rains and May,
the glade of the wood, that girl from Breckon.

★

There on the tide, bright
as snow, as salt and the sun,
the moon-white gull fishes.
It is like a lily light on the waves;
or a nun; or paper, white
for writing; or my letter to a girl. So go now.
Find camp and castle, that girl bright

144

as Arthur's mother, and say these words,
say that she must say *yes*, that Dafydd dies,
gentle Dafydd, unless he has his way.
Neither Taliesin nor burning Merlin,
magical with girls, loved one prettier.
Oh what color! Those copper cheeks,
the loveliest in Christendom. Oh my God!
Tell her to hurry, to be sweet, to agree
or that girl will be the death of me.

★

Modest Morvith of the golden hair,
that lily-browed girl in Enid's shape,
made passion catch and glow to flame
when in bright leaves once around my neck
her white arms went to take me slave
to lips I'd not known. And now by love's knot
I'm bound as by her arms, white as winter,
when face to face, when sin was simple,
she thralled me down in the brown-bright leaves.
But a collar shy and smooth as arms is slavery
I could take. Arms white as lime are gifts
on any neck. And hers seem torques of gold
and blinding spells, bright beauty's famed design.
And I, blond Dafydd, the wine-bred bard, am bolder boy
for having known them there, and without care
and drunk on her—my slim, my strong,
my Morvith of the golden hair.

★

Under the green hazels this morning
I heard a thrush sing verses bright as visions.
Morvith, my golden girl from Caer, had sent him here
full of song to sing in Nentyrch dingle.

May-flowers and the green wings of the wind
cloaked him like a priest. And everywhere
was all cathedral. And it was, by God, as if
the altar's roof was pure gold. And then
May's child and music's master
in shining language chanting declared
the gospel: a leaf as Host, and sanctus bell
by nightingale. And as this mass was said
and rose above the hedge, they raised to God
their chaliced liveliness and love. And here
in this grove, I was gladdened by song.

★

Duthgie, brilliant, shining Duthgie
of darkest, smoothest hair, come
lie down with me in Manafan dingle.
No cheap food I'll spread
but no glutton's feast nor reaper's meal,
nor farmer's fare nor lean and Lenten meat
or English meal. Gold girl, I'll serve you
mead and song, a nightingale's cry and thrush's cheer,
a hidden thicket, a birchen bower. And while in leaves we lie,
the trees will lean to shade our joys.
There birds ride branches, and nine fine trees
will round our rest; above is blue,
and below is clover soft as heaven's flour.
There two—or even three—can lie. In the wild
where oat-raised roebuck ride, where blackbirds
are thick and trees are bright and beggars can't find us,
where hawks are nursed and air is sweet and water cool, there
where passion is frequent and heaven's right now,
that's our place, my honey girl. Tonight, tonight,
you ember-eyed, wave-bright beauty. Duthgie, hurry;
we've things to do.

★

Until I saw a mirror, I'd never known
I was not so fine and fair. My God,
yellow cheeks, a nose like a razor. Terrible!
My eager eyes looked like dumb holes,
my hair—a bunch of weeds!
It might have been a trick, a magic mirror
made of lies, but that would make the world
more strange than even I had thought.
Yet if it's true I might as well be dead
for all my looks are likely to get me.
Goddamn mirror! Dark, blue, moon-glowing
and brightening like charm-work.
It works mortals the way magnets work metal.
Witch-made mirror, swift changing dream,
cold traitor and brother to the frost, go rot in hell!
But if I *am* as haggard as all that, it's the fault
of those girls from Gwynedd. Damn those Gwynedd girls,
so beautiful, so unobliging, so skilled
at spoiling the fine features of a boy.

★

God damn the girls of this parish!
I'm so horny I'm bent double.
I haven't even had a hag, much less
a wife or virgin in I don't know how long. What's with 'em!
What harm would it do some brown-browed girl
to lead me to the woods and lie down
in shadowed leaves? I'm always in love
and no curse clings worse. Daily I see girls
I'd die for but am no nearer getting
than if they hated me. On Sundays
I go churching but twist from God
to face the fine-faced girls of Llandbadarn.
"Look at the good-looking boy,"

one beauty whispers, "He might be fun."
"Forget it," says the bitch with her,
"that's Dafydd, a real creep,
a gawker. And take a look at that nose."
No more dazed looks for her! I might even become a hermit now,
but I couldn't help turning, couldn't help
staring at such shining. I've learned my stern lesson,
I, strong song's stout friend: I'll bow my head
and go out alone—at least today, at least from this room.

★

Yesterday I waited out the rain
under a green birch, stood in the wet
waiting on a girl because I'm a damn fool,
but Gwen's face could also launch ships
and make grown men eager as boys.
But it slipped quick as I could sign the cross
when some shaded thing loomed up saying,
Be silent, Dafydd; I,
always naked beside you, am your shadow-self
come to show you—dare you look—your self.
Myself! You? You look like a scarecrow!
Did some jealous husband pay you for this?
You're nothing of me. Look,
I'm young; I'm blond; look at these looks,
you hag-shanked ghost-herder;
bog heron; muck smeared humpback
with a saint-face and lusty look.
Take care, Dafydd; I shadow you everywhere,
lie down with your trysts and shade your lies,
know enough to ruin you well enough.
Well, then let the devil shit you, shade.
I've killed no dogs, no hens with hurling-stones,
scared no children, given no girls

cause for complaint. *But what if I said you had,*
why there'd be whole villages of rage,
and then: a missing poet. "Dafydd, you say?
No I haven't seen him for days"; "Dafydd, oh yes,
last month"; "Dafydd, yes, I think I remember him,
a poet, wasn't he?" Then sew up your lips
to what faults I have shadow-self. You need me
more than I you, old creep. And though I may lie
to lie with Gwen, you, too, will rise and fall and rise again.

★

When food and frolic's the thing we're after,
a Welshman's got the longest nose. So,
though the town was new, I quickly found
a lively inn and called for wine. And then
I saw her! Oh God! So slender, so rare;
so rare and slender I ordered roast
and old wine and called her to my bench.
She was shy, but not for long with such a feast
and the stuff I whispered. She said *sure*
and I said *soon as everyone's asleep.*
And then I just thought about her eyes,
dark as her hair and soon to be mine.
Naturally it got screwed up. I bumped the beds,
fell, bruised my leg, hit my shin on a stool,
then ran scared into a table, knocked off a bowl,
got the dogs abarking, and to top it off
stumbled into three crummy Englishmen
in one stinking bed, peddlers: Hicken, Shenkin, and Shack,
or some such names. And one of those scum-mouthed bastards
started yelling, "A Welshman's creeping about;
hold tight to your purses." That got everybody up,
and I, Dafydd, poet, lover, with headache and shin-ache
had to crouch around trembling like a thief.

But I prayed, and thanks to Jesus and all the saints
got back to bed hoping God forgives
the sins we suffer for slim and slender girls.

★

That glorious girl who holds her court
in the grove would never guess
what I'd confessed to the mouse-gray friar.
I went to say my sin: that I was a poet
and idolatrous at that, for there's a girl!
Ah, dark-browed and bright-faced, a girl
I worship, I want, I haven't had,
my murderer, whose praise I've carried
and loveliness lyricked the whole of Wales,
without success. I want her in bed
between me and the wall. And so the friar said,
"Don't waste yourself in lust
for a paper-pale and foam-white face;
think of Judgment Day, think
of your soul. And quit the verse;
God didn't die for you to write poetry!
And that stuff you write! Fol de rol and rot;
stirs up the kids, gives them ideas.
Dafydd, you could damn down your soul
with such sensual rhyme." But I told him,
"God's not as mean as you'd have Him be.
He wouldn't damn a boy for loving gently,
since women are what the world loves best,
are heaven's fairest flowers—next to God, of course.
Every joy is heaven made, and misery's hell's domain.
You've got to preach; I've got to write.
And I've as much a right to sing for bread
as you to beg those loaves. Your hymns and psalms
are also poems, Friar. Not with one food alone God feeds

150

the world. There's time to pray and preach,
make song and sing, as well. Poems are sung at feasts
to please the girls, and prayers are saved for church
to gain a different grace. Good friar,
when men are as ready to hear *paters*
as they are to hear harpers,
and Gwynedd girls beg my wanton lays,
I swear to pray for nights and days.
But till that day, there's shame on me
if I sing any hymns but poetry."

Here in Louisiana

Here in Louisiana it is December now.
The eaves are free and even. The blank sky hangs here
and seems to wait. Late bananas
are beginning to turn, may even be
ready before the frost stops their sweetening.
Still, this weather winters a few leaves brown,
drives some birds still further south,
and forces roaches beneath the loose bark of live oaks
or deep into the fronds of palms, under old planks
or here and there in the warmer dark.

Today I realized I'd not seen one in weeks.
We live with them here, with their presumption
and prowls, casually, as casually
as we live with humidity and small craft warnings,
with our governors and hurricanes.
They don't distress us quite like they
distress others. And our complaints are resigned,
informal, furyless. Such small, quick acts of God
racing out over kitchen counters
are too fast for more concern—or swatters, usually.

Cracked, they stir more disgust than let alone
to romp over cake crumbs and clean plates:
being big as thumbs,
broken, such things spill their creamy thickness
like salves or clots or rancid lotions.
And unless ground to grease
some brown fragment will twitch for a day or more
till others clean the carapace to pristine silence.

And so we usually leave them alone,
wait on winter to pretty our kitchens,

forget them till Spring, till camellias return
and wisteria twines the fences of South Louisiana,
covers clotheslines, the backs of greenhouses and garages,
drifts over bayous and fields and out toward the Gulf,
the waves and spray, till on fragrant, rainless evenings
out on walks we hear a stirring, what seems at first a fine,
faint mist striking the scattered leaves.

Voyages into Summer

Nothing much moves here
now, and summer has stretched over
south Louisiana like a canvas tent.
You feel it collect against you,
thumbs and fat hands of heat,
thick mobs of weighted air.
People stay in.
Streets quieten down.
Cats grow lean, lie flat
as death and oblivious
to the heat-braved plumps
of food and feathers
pecking for grass seed,
for slow bugs
right in front of them.

But for their foraging
most everything has stopped now.
Even the clocks slow down.
Yet in these barely moving hours,
these warm, slow minutes
a pure and sensual excess stirs.

The air turns perfume—
rose, gardenia and grasses,
and even the vines
low hanging from the oaks.
And everything is more green,
more bright than any other time.

To walk here through the heart of summer
where whole towns have turned hot houses

and even the dirt, the molds, the mushrooms
of old stumps lift up their spice somehow
to float in the still steam of this air,
steam hung, unrising within the tent of summer,
drives all senses thrilling
into luxury, into the warm calm,
and slow breath
of the voluptuous.

In Silver Season

Even winter moves south,
and the days darken
in their darkling tumble
toward the solstice.
Cold falls out of the air
and evening comes quicker now.
All the heavy,
honey-drunk scents
of grass, vine, and mold,
of flowers that famish for heat
have gone. And nothing rides
upon the air but dinner
slipping out back doors
opened to let the cat in
or let the cat out.
What's in the air
is thrift; it's penury
and miserliness.
Everything rich is broke—
dried, fragile, or gone.

But out on the lake
in the snowless grey
of barely freezing dusk
one can sometimes see
dark heron diving,
can hear cold waters
breaking in spangled sacrifice,
in communion as extravagant,
as silvered, as munificent
as the seasons' flash and circuit.

The Surrounding Grace

I've nothing clever to say
about this
most ordinary of events,
a progress
common as desire.

Had some strange, bright wish,
the kind that fames out
one's wit and name, occurred,
I'd have wished it
for this flesh
fragile as a yolk,
these bones
finer than a quail's.

But none did, and so
I find the wish I wish
in a cliché, the third of a cliché,
the dullest prose: I hope
my child will be healthy.
Money I can give it,
and happiness finally
is always singular.

I'm nearly forty, though,
accustomed to myself,
to wife, work and the stuff
of routine. And now
to let swim into my address
and concern a thing
to worry up whole years,
decades, the rest

of what I've got
is need's strangest
quirking of me yet.

Time, that soil of lust,
of greed's multiplication,
may set us apart, wither
love down, and make you dream
of other fathers, other names.
But I'd have you difficult
and dark, as hateful
as my parents said I was,
to having you sweet
and slow, unable to catch
the strange, bitter grace
you soon will enter into.

A Crown of Promise

FOR DAFYDD

I. Poem Concluding with a Line from Euripides

My son restores what time has taken.
The past is gathered up full-fleshed,
incarnadined now whole and hallowed,
returned in processions from the soured stone and mold.
And this is rapture,
time's fullness in aureate blossom,
the kingdom and promise of pearl. My father and grandmother
rise, and my mother is elixered back
into her agile joy. The air is pungent
with pear, with lemon yeast,
and the goods of gardens.
And nothing but anger is alien as he
or is it I lie in the quilts
of our parents' great bed
complete, singing, and oblivious
to the bones of fear.
O God, Beast, Mystery, come.

II. The Things I Would Tell My Son of Gods, Beasts, and Mystery

Be in no hurry to find them.
Let them seek you if they will.
Their sport is play,
and there is always time.
No fires wait the loiterer,

no blackened angelic grotesques,
no lack of joy. Trust this
as you would the strength of my arms,
as you would your mother's love, and know
a sure crazing will claim the eyes
and atomize the sight,
will stun down to gabble
the tongues of those who intrude
the sacred wood. Whole lives,
complete and wholly blest, can pass
without mystery. Life's gift comes
with no demands, and love alone
is all the duty we need know.

III. The Duty of Love

When I am shadow stuff again
and vague as my mother's dream of me
before my birth, alive only
in the communion of ancestors,
in the unshakable chemistry at the depth
of your cells, or arcing in the fire
of your brain, or rippling outward
in some perpetuating kindness of my hand—
or cruelty or accident—
and when your mother, too, has grown vague,
her voice unrecallable, her face
clear and exact only in snap-shot,
only on old vacations or the starts of school,
on birthdays as blown from your memory
as past wishes, the days
she and I could not bear to leave or let
to memory's thoughtless slide,

then see us in some face
you've come to hate,
or having fled those traps of fear,
in eyes you'd not think ours, lips
you'd not wish on yours. See us there, Dafydd,
there alone, whole and restored.

Gifts

τὰ μεγάλα δῶρα τῆς Τύχης ἔχει φόβον

They do not befall us without price,
the great gifts: the five-foot check
delivered as the cameras roll—
and roll on into our lives until
everything is spent; the easy buttons,
the easy kisses and easy thighs of girls
whose veins have not yet risen
to the bumpy maps of their futures—
and their quick, their easy dependencies
hard as lawyers' teeth;
the big house, the big car, the big boat—
bigger debts, bigger dents, bigger leaks.

Unfortunately, such stuff of dream and fear
does too often descend
to tingle our monotonous days
into pure expectancy. Debt and apathy
are relieved, desire inflamed,
and all our assorted greeds are blent
to the brown nausea of hope.

Even revelation sometimes falls
with such a swiftness
and leaves us cleansed, brightened,
gowned in light, or so it seems,
till we come back or till our graceful fitting
turns perpetual and our eyes shut
to dirt, stain, spittle, crust,
and all the other leavings of ecstasy.

And so I try to pray
for nothing, try wanting nothing
but the simple gifts that fall—
the sight of goslings
the size of my fist diving,
diving for the bread falling
from the hands of my son.

Written on My Fiftieth Birthday

I awake this morning,
this second day of January
now fifty-one times having come round
and fallen on my shoulders, awake
with the revolving zodiac's reproach
and rise with all its cumulative anger
calculating me closer to extinction.
How the very syllables of the word—of *fifty*—
ring like a lead bell to thud the day
and hang on me like excess fat,
accustomed aches and indigestion,
and all the accumulation of time, error, and mistake.

But—to hell with the goat's celestial buckings.
Go off. Come round. Return. I accept the years.
From now on, Capricorn, it's welcome back.
At such a turning as this one,
none's left to ring so ominous.
I'll take each new one now
as accident, as blessing, as joy,
as an unencumbered gift
of the circuiting stars.

The Song That You Are Watching

Vain is man who glories in his joys without fear, while all about him the chances of the years dance like an idiot in the wind.

Euripides

The livid silver tongues of the early stars leaped between the shapes of the chimney-pots, backwards and forwards, like idiot children dancing to a forgotten tune.

Stella Gibbons

. . . the pleasure of looking and the pleasure of seeing, like watching people dancing through an open window. They seem a little mad at first until you realize they hear the song that you are watching.

Sam Wagstaff

Hand in hand we idiots jump and jog
doing our dumb shows
beneath the stars,
laughing with the tunes
we know we think we hear,
songs to mock
those sure and certain fates
spun out to fall—
the old destinies:
age, disease, decay.

Of course babies are shattered in wars,
and children sometimes witness
a nastiness that lingers into decades
souring day by day what joy might have been,
and good men die young.

That the unspeakable might slip into our lives
and stuff our mouths with its dirt

or rip away the legs to break
our idiot gaits and bring us down
is still no cause for doric doom and despair.

And Sophocles, too, was wrong,
wrong as the lot of them.
To weigh all days against the last
denies good idiot sense.
Joy is in the dance that's danced,
the songs you hear but others only watch,
and all the things that turn to dust.
Count as happy those who dance the most.

Spring Wind: Meditation on a Line from the Ninth Eclogue of Virgil and a Contrary Meditation on a Line from Whitman

I

Omnia fert aetas; animum quoque.

We've all watched them,
the sickening regressions,
seen mothers forget our names,
heard fathers call us Daddy,
known neighbors
who just wandered off.

Time is wind
fragmenting down to elementals
everything,

dispersing substance
back to the raws.

The years whip
and tornado through
rock and wood,
twist steel easy as meat.

We watch golden boys
gone off the promise,
poems gone to prose
or worse,
bewildered old women

with hands dirty as their coats—
all carried off.

Pure subtraction
everywhere
years and age bearing it off,
brains popping like cheap bulbs.

Wind and years
and all the mathematics of regret,
the pathologies of old desire.

Age carries the years
carry off everything off,
off even off the mind off
off off off!

II

Life, life is the tillage, and Death is the harvest according.

Off, yes, yes, everything,
even the mind—harvested,
like a bushel of turnips,

but clear thought in a body gone
ripe as good cheese
is worse, is pure Poe:
that rising wall of brick;
or waking up too well dressed in a bed too tight
in a room too small.

Oh, let the diminishments fall,
the dumb, unfocused stares and stupid words:
yes, I used to write—recipes, I think;

let them go hand in spotted hand
with my drool, my dotter, my odor,
my stuck smile of a man gone off
on vacation to hula-hula isles.

So what! that we're finally subtracted
out of what was mostly tillage, mostly addition.

Nothing but flesh
I'd prefer to have housed
these loins in, to have held
music and water sound
and certain words, held light and shade,
and made record of certain times
in certain arms.

And even stone is finally effaced
in such long blowing wind.

I can feel it beginning to stir,
just around my feet now, sometimes
feel its updrafts.

But all the bad lines, the steaming piles
of stupidities, lies and little cruelties,
they, too, are stirring,
will lift someday, rise up and also vanish
in the Spring's warm, according, and redemptive wind.

In Primary Light

FOR CAROL

In Maine's broad and bronzing light—
in lemon pungence, brazen
and honeyed, full as wheat and amber's
wide ranging—in such light spangling down
along its bouldered shore,
its water-shined and barnacled stone
my son and I climbed hand in hand
and watched between quick tides
the minerals' flicker beneath the Atlantic's
thin receding, the stones' lightning dry
before a wet hand or returning tide
caressed berylliums and micas to again bronze out
like Maine's summer light.

And doing only this and that
we talked of black-green pods,
the sand-studded weed and wood, and shell
the color of a boy's rose cheeks
in this Maine light, and the wide
relaxing light, the light itself,
more calm than lower light,
than palm and live oak light,
and talked of what tomorrow we'd find:
a glistening of seals, the thunder rock,
and nothing but such things as this,
this idle stuff that dances time,
all time turning, light to dark to light to dark,
time twirling in its repeating wheel,
that turns even the dumbest ticking of jagged gears
into a gloried and lambent joy.

★ ★ ★

Man in splendor's no easy concept now,
and Europe's green is made fertile with flesh.
At the wheat's root burns
what was once a child.
It is shame we sickle to mill
and shame we break to eat.
This is the loam of children,
the humus of their voices.
Such earth cannot credence the lie
of renewals and returns
and death the warm mother.
There is no return,
no warmth but the compost's,
no good come from our time.
The earth is not increased;
nothing is renewed;
everything is lessened.

Time's turned carrion-keeper in our time,
the clerk of cruelty
ledgering-in libraries of the unspeakable,
but you would not think it so,
would not doubt the splendid
were you here on this coast with me this morning
watching my son watching the cold tides
in light breathing out over the bay.

★ ★ ★

From my window and through the sway
of old ecru I see them on the shore,
children who at such distance seem
slips and moving brights of color
carrying their pails and shells, busy
with sand's easy commerce.

Such scenes seem at such remove
from the branchings desire will take:
the minking up of the thighs, the sleek,
acrid heat of inflorescence and yearning;
blond boys' crownings out in the rerouting
of joys. But I'd wish innocence
on no one but children, would not hold
from my son the frenzy and driving
or desire's assumption of the heart,
biology turned mystery, the heavy paws
of need, and the incomprehensible lexicon
of lust; haze and indistinction, slips
rippling behind curtains, bafflement
at having been led till now by purpose,
led to a clear shore with sparkling sand.

★ ★ ★

All Maine's mornings are not alike,
not swept with the possibilities of red
above a harbor balancing miles of bright
fragmented foil on the undulating breath of the Atlantic.
In some there is a quickening in the light and air,
a brightness and cold flashing,
like the lifting of sails in the wind
and the wind's catching of white
and the rapid riding out;
the full speed of men fluent in knots
looping the thick ropes like kite strings
winding and whipping them into language
in the numbed, platinum light
of descended clouds and silent sun.

★ ★ ★

Last night spanning out in slow glide,
gulls dipped and called. The moon
spangled down, flared from the orange rouge
of old ladies smelling of talc, their lips
fragrant with glycerin and rose water,
to a pure blazing—intense as lead just cooled,
while lilac in fade and flame on the air recalled
the thin linen of ladies' handkerchiefs,
so thick with scent they tumbled
to the cool bottoms of black purses
big as Bibles, tumbled
with gloves and currency to wait,
to be drawn out, to infuse the air
like that lilac'd cool that came
coursing in with tides and gulls
and memories of my grandmother,
who would have given whole years
to have been here for a moment
just to have put her hand
into his golden, moon-marked curls.

★ ★ ★

There is another Maine.
It also curves the shore
in generous and prospering light.
But it is not the same;
this is the Maine of outlet stores
and flea markets, of miles of shacks of junk
all clustering the same glittering shore.

Green brontosaurs rear up from miniature golf courses
and peer out at the highway; tipsy lobsters
bow-tied and in tails dance on the sides
of highway bars; and giant bears

atop concrete waterfalls look down
at the rows of campers rolling up
from America into Maine.

Into the ideal the tawdry always intrudes;
the hills of wild lupines give way;
the shore lines give way;
the delicate bays surrender their charm.

In the amusement park by the zoo
where I take my son, I watch
bumper cars collide and tattooed kids
fondle each other. His hand
is under her blouse; she rubs
her middle finger along his zipper.
They're both so unwashed
there's no thrill to watching.

My son pets the Vietnamese pot-bellied pigs.
For a quarter he gets a handful of feed.
Signs encourage children to feed the animals.
A deer too full to rise sits and lets him stroke
its fuzzing antlers. It does not like
the feel of a child's fingers on its tender horn,
jerks its head but does not rise.

Nothing here in this Maine rises
once having settled in. The lupines
are mowed and paved over; the chestnuts' flambeaux
extinguished in their fellings; the rhododendron
graveled down. All that lifts into the air here
is the smell of grease and batter. Nothing
will rise again. This is the Maine
bent to Mammon, that peels and cracks
and is replastered and repainted
so brontosaurs and bears can forever stare down,

lobsters frolic, and new pigs and deer
be brought in when the others' arteries
squeeze shut, and no one notices, and no one
notices that anything has changed,
that anything has ever changed.

★ ★ ★

Þe tyme þat ic in lijf has lende
in idel-nes ic haue it spende.

from Cursor Mundi, a
Northumbrian poem, ca. 1300

Here where light and lilac,
air and bouldered shore meld
to mark the coast of Maine,
and beauty's lyric and blossoming,
the three of us in idle light
toy with time, dare tides to touch
our feet, and wander green streets
where architecture is precise as the air
and chestnuts in Amazonian abundance
outflower Provence; here where time's
at our wills' wishing in bright and idle light,
I wonder who with more talent for metaphor
than happiness first cast the grand equation,
first felt he'd spent or wasted joy's doing,
believed it convertible to coin or ash, saw time
as money, and thought days in lilac light
might be bettered in prayer or commerce.
Some Larkinesque medieval, I guess.
And I can hear him with his "What about
Mondays" and "What'll you do when
the vacation's over?"—To set the present
against the future, to make time joy's spoiler

is like a taste for birch and leather, a vice
and misery there seems no casting out
of those for whom happiness is gall and boredom.

★ ★ ★

In primary light things are clarified;
knowledge is optic and immediate,
so obvious its utterance is commonplace:
as when I watched my son being born
and knew the truth of a hundred tritenesses;
or that day I lifted him and dislocated
his shoulder and felt fear and frenzy
with a knotting thick as fists; or when we sat
beneath a cool purity of light
and I watched him toss the largest stones
he could lift and call my attention
to each splash, and I remembered another beach,
another . . . oh, the obvious, the obvious:
when I remembered that love and light equate,
and that in this incandescence he kindles
I am defined, that in such definition,
such a showering of clear light,
I see billions of girls and boys
in his brilliant and burnished curls.

Self Portrait after Stanley Spencer

You have no idea how hard it is to live out
a great romance.

                                        Wallis Windsor

1.

It's not so difficult, really.
And I'd guess that plowing
or the laying of brick,
row on row, or the securing
of a steel axle might damage
more of some fine genealogical
delicacy or comfortable ease
than all love's labors compounded.

It's not so difficult, I think.
Attending enslaves only the selfish.
And joy is the product of stability's
clockwork. The monotonous grinding
of love's gears perpetually renews.
Ecstasy can be cultivated
like peas: Mendels of love
made free in the laws of attendance.

2.

In the abundance of her flesh and help
she stretches the length of the canvas,
secures edges, sees to his centering,
and holds more than half his gaze.
He watches his toys float in space,
thinks himself haloed in the *et ceteras*

of his obsessions. But in her solid span
they are dwarfed down to nothing,
and the viewer is unaware even
of the brown paint-outs, the receding shadows.
Here is a man born to luck.
The ability to paint out the heart's slough
is his luck. She is his luck,
and her attendance is his keeping and his joy.

3.

Jacketed, ear-muffed, and gloved,
I'd go into the garden
to drive my grandmother's pitchfork
into the frozen ground
between the hydrangeas. I'd pull up
thick chunks of earth
to taste the ice that had crystaled
inches down in the dark. And I'd dig
and play until I'd hear my grandmother's knuckles
against the steamed window panes
of her kitchen calling me in.

It's January again, and I am perhaps now
half done with this accidental blessing.
A bead of sweat this moment drips down
from the kitchen window. The child
still turns the frozen earth. The grandmother
still calls him in. Everything
is gone; everything is whole;
everything is blessed.

for Carol

NOTES

The Comeback of Yma Sumac

Peruvian singer Yma Sumac, whose real name was not Amy Camus, despite all myths to the contrary, appeared in the 1954 B-movie *Secret of the Incas*, filmed, as I recall, at Macchu Picchu, and made a record entitled *Voice of the Xtabay* which illustrated her bizarre four octave vocal range. In the eighties *Vogue* ran a short notice of her New York comeback. Her recordings are still available today, and there is even an "official" Yma Sumac webpage.

How Little Lillian Found the Lord and Served Him

The Cowper quotation is from his poem "The Castaway."

How I Tried to Explain the Certainties of Faith and Petrunkevitch's Famous Essay on the Wasp and the Tarantula to a Pentecostal Student Worried about My Soul

cf. Alexander Petrunkevitch, "The Spider and the Wasp," first published in 1952 in *Scientific American*.

About Their Father's Business

Jubilate Agno (Rejoice in the Lamb) is a long, religious poem by Christopher Smart, a mad eighteenth-century poet. The most well-known section is a rhapsodic and religious meditation on his cat. Brendan, Irish explorer saint and discoverer of America; Plenty, Terry, *et al.*, newspaper comic strip characters.

Locomotion and Starlight

Much of the vocabulary here comes from the world of railroading, of engineers, firemen, breakmen, switchmen, and call boys, who fire, break, switch, and call.

Star Washer

Much of the poem's imagery derives, though somewhat obliquely, from the work of the great American photographer Keith Carter.

The Last Model

Baron Wilhelm von Gloeden (1856–1931) was the first great photographer of the male nude.

The Mysteries: Elegy at Century's Close

I. The Symbol, *cf.* Max Klinger's cycle of etchings *Ein Handschub* (*A Glove*).

Meditative Stanzas: On Stanley Spencer

Particular paintings by Spencer are not relevant to the poem. II:1, *cf.* Luke 1:18; "and spring the leg that leaps the womb," *cf.* Luke 1:41; III, water and fire, *cf.* Luke 3:16.

Sacred Celebrations for the Moon's Beginning: Five Menarcheal Songs with Epigraphs from St. Simeon

Menarche, Gk., literally, the beginning of the moon. This is St. Simeon the New Theologian, the mystic and poet, not St. Simeon Stylites. *Akathist* in the Greek Church is a song of thanksgiving. In the Middle Ages Cupid was sometimes revered as a saint.

The Honey of Hellas

cf. W. B. Yeats' translation of the chorus in "Colonus' Praise " from *Oedipus at Colonus* in *The Tower; cf.* Hart Crane's "Voyages."

ἡ ποιητική

i.e., the poetics, the art of poetry.

Homage to Dafydd ap Gwilym

Dafydd ap Gwilym, a contemporary of Chaucer and Boccaccio, was born at Bro Gynin, near Aberystwyth, around the year 1320, and he is thought to have died around 1380. He was the greatest Welsh bard of the middle ages. *Homage*, prepared as a gift for my son, is a loose, free, but artistically faithful translation after some of his major poems arranged so as to suggest, if not his biography exactly, at least his primary concerns and passions.

Voyages into Summer

cf. Baudelaire's *"L'Invitation au voyage."*

Gifts

τὰ μεγάλα δῶρα τῆς Τύχης ἔχει φόβον, *i.e.*, "The great gifts come with fear." *cf.* the Shaker hymn "Simple Gifts."

The Song That You Are Watching

The first epigraph is taken from Hecuba's speech following the brutal murder of her grandson in *The Trojan Women;* the second is from *Cold Comfort Farm*, a novel in which a character's life is ruined by something she once saw; the last is from *A Book of Photographs* by a great collector who was a victim of AIDS.

About the Author

John Wood holds professorships in both photographic history and English literature at McNeese University in Lake Charles, Louisiana, where he is also director of the Master of Fine Arts Program in Creative Writing. He is the author of three previous books of poetry and seven books of art and photographic criticism. His books have won the Iowa Poetry Prize twice, the American Photographic Historical Society's Outstanding Book of the Year Award, the American Library Association's *Choice* Outstanding Academic Books of 1992, and the *New York Times Book Review* Best Photo Books of 1995. He co-curated the landmark 1995 Smithsonian Institution exhibition *Secrets of the Dark Chamber* and is editor of *21st: The Journal of Contemporary Photography, Culture and Criticism*.

DATE DUE

JAN 5 '00 F		
NOV 2 7 1999		